KU-012-919

Psychology for the Classroom: Constructivism and Social Learning

Alan Pritchard and John Woollard

Routledge
Taylor & Francis Group

LONDON AND NEW YORK

First published 2010
by Routledge
2 Park Square, Milton Park, Abingdon, Oxon, OX14 4RN

Simultaneously published in the USA and Canada
by Routledge
270 Madison Avenue, New York, NY 10016

Routledge is an imprint of the Taylor & Francis Group, an informa business

© 2010 Alan Pritchard and John Woollard

Typeset in Bembo by Swales & Willis Ltd, Exeter, Devon
Printed and bound in Great Britain by CPI Antony Rowe, Chippenham, Wiltshire

British Library Cataloguing in Publication Data
A catalogue record for this book is available from the British Library

Library of Congress Cataloging-in-Publication Data
Pritchard, Alan (Alan M.)
  Psychology for the classroom : constructivism and social learning /
Alan Pritchard and John Woollard.
      p. cm. — (Psychology for the classroom series)
    Includes bibliographical references.
  1. Constructivism (Education).   2. Learning, Psychology of.   3. Group
work in education.   4. Computer-assisted instruction.   5. Effective teaching.
  I. Woollard, John.   II. Title.
  LB1590.3.P77 2010
  370.15′23—dc22   2009038617

ISBN10: 0–415–49479–6 (hbk)
ISBN10: 0–415–49480–X (pbk)
ISBN10: 0–203–85517–5 (ebk)

ISBN13: 978–0-415–49479–3 (hbk)
ISBN13: 978–0-415–49480–9 (pbk)
ISBN13: 978–0-203–85517–1 (ebk)

Contents

Figures

Preface

The focus of this series of books is the psychological elements of educational practice. The series aims to draw together and elucidate, at more than a superficial level, the major current topics of concern that are related to learning and to other important areas of psychological interest.

In the past teachers in training were introduced, at an entry level at least, to some of the psychology of learning and education. Although this element of the UK teacher training curriculum (TDA, 2007) has not quite disappeared completely, there is a considerably reduced emphasis placed on it in teacher training than was previously the case. Teachers currently in post report that they were not introduced satisfactorily to what they consider important aspects of learning – theory in particular – during their training (Pritchard, 2005). The relative success of *Ways of Learning* (Pritchard, 2005, 2009), and other books dealing with the same subject matter, can be seen as indicative of a need for more psychology for teachers and teachers in training.

In support of the wider rationale for the series, the work of Burton and Bartlett (2006) has some important points to make. They suggest that there is a danger that new ideas for pedagogical approaches in the classroom are often promoted, sometimes by government agencies, without the detailed research and theoretical underpinning relating to it being considered with due diligence:

> The speed with which the internet and television can transmit ideas and information and appear to afford them (often spurious) validation should concern us as educators . . . [they are concerned that] high-profile education consultants deliver courses on new pedagogies . . . [the presentations are] . . . drawn eclectically from a range of research findings thought to have practical benefits for learning [and that teachers] generally enjoy these stimulating sessions and the recipe approach to pedagogic

techniques but they are not encouraged to look deeper into the research that underpins them.

(Burton and Bartlett, 2006: 44–45)

The books in this series aim to provide the opportunity, in an accessible and relevant way, to enable teachers, teachers in training and others with a professional interest in children, classrooms and learning to look more deeply at topics, background research and potential efficacy and to be able to make choices about their own pedagogical approaches and preferences from a position of knowledge and understanding. The authors will consider the needs of those in training to be teachers and are required to examine the theoretical and research basis for their teaching practice. This is important as it is increasingly the case that courses leading to Qualified Teacher Status (QTS) are linking assessed work to expectations of a master's level and awarding credits towards master's degrees. This is particularly the case with postgraduate-level teacher training courses.

The series, in turn, presents and examines the detail and potential of a range of psychology-related topics in the light of their value and usefulness for practising teachers. Each of the authors in this series presents an outline of the topic, a review of the research which underpins its principles, the implications of the underpinning theory for pedagogy and a consideration of strategies which teachers might employ if they wish to implement the precepts of theory in their teaching. The books aim to outline a trail from research and theory, to pedagogy and thence to teaching strategies in practice. There is a clear pedagogical element to the books. They present the ideas in the perspectives of research, theory, pedagogy and strategies for teaching. There are suggestions for further reading and activities, both of which are written to develop understanding and are classroom-based to develop skills and knowledge. The more general strategies provide teachers with sound starting points for developing their own particular plans for lessons and series of lessons including activities which will be informed by the principles of the topic in question.

Research is presented and explored; the theory generated by the research is outlined; and the pedagogical implications of the theory, leading to teaching strategies, follow. Within a set, but flexible, framework, individual authors have written in a way suited both to the requirements of teachers in training and the interests of teachers in practice.

Part of the intention of the series is to look beyond the charisma of the presenters of day courses, and similar, for teachers (Burton and Bartlett, 2006) and beyond the showy and commercialised publications aimed at selling expensive materials. Each book aims to give an evidence-based consideration of the possibilities afforded by new findings and ideas, a review of research upon which claims for teaching efficacy have been built and a solid foundation for teachers and those in training to build their own ideas and strategies. The new ideas and findings are presented in the context of existing knowledge, understanding and practice of the topic in question.

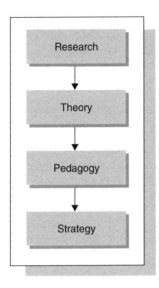

Figure 0.1 The conceptual path taken by each author when writing

Acknowledgements

We would like to say thanks for the contributions made by classroom teachers Claire Johnson, Catherine Richards, Lesley Scopes and Cynthia Selby, the virtual contributions made by Light Sequent and Stradd Ling and the contributions made by colleagues at the University of Warwick and the University of Southampton.

This book is dedicated, with heartfelt thanks, to our offspring, Maria, Frances, Mattie and Becky. Watching them grow, socialise and learn opened our eyes and helped us begin to understand how it all seems to work.

1 Introduction

By the end of this chapter you will be able to:

■ contextualise the constructivist movement and understand its place in the scheme of psychological theory related to learning.

And you will have:

■ considered the beginnings of constructivist learning theory;
■ been given an overview of the social constructivist approach to theory;
■ been given and considered an introduction to social constructivist ideas and to some of its proponents;
■ been given an overview of related social learning theories developed by such people as Bandura, and Lave and Wenger.

The aim of this book is to introduce the background and theory of social constructivism and social learning theory, to show how the theory might be translated into a set of pedagogical approaches to the teaching curriculum and to show how the pedagogy might be developed into practical strategies and activities for teachers to consider and deploy in their teaching.

In order to meet the first of these aims, it is important, possibly for social constructivist reasons (which will become clearer as the book develops), to situate social constructivism in the wider context of constructivist learning theory and also in the even wider context of constructivist thought and philosophy, which extends beyond learning into other areas of social, ethical and psychological thought.

An introduction to the constructivist movement

Mahoney (2005) tells us that the terms "constructivism", "constructivist" and other related words and phrases have only recently become a part of the psychological lexicon. By "recently" he means from the beginning of the second half of the twentieth century. However, he traces the underlying ideas, though largely embryonic in nature, back a good deal further. There is a history of two thousand years attached to constructivist thought in the Eastern tradition and a history of at least three hundred years in Western thought.

Walsh (1999) cites the writing of Gautama Buddha (560–477 BC): "We are what we think. All that we are arises within our thoughts. With our thoughts we make the world" (45). This is indeed the view that individuals construct the world in which they live. That is, we come to understand our surroundings through processes of thinking based upon what is observed or otherwise experienced. More of this will come later.

Heraclitus (c.535–474 BC), a pre-Socratic philosopher, has also been shown to be a very early constructivist-style thinker. Most famously, Heraclitus is known for saying that we cannot step into the same river twice. Kirk (1986) suggests that Heraclitus drew distinction between "an 'inner' state of beliefs and an 'outer' state of facts, accessible to anyone" (62). This seems to be saying that the facts of the outer world are interpreted by the individual to form the beliefs of the individual's version of reality. This is, as we will see, a constructivist view on reality and the individual.

The founder of Taoism, Lao Tzu, a contemporary of Gautama Buddha, more or less, also made statements to the effect that reality is a changing and variable entity which can be perceived differently by different individuals.

In the Western context, Giambattista Vico (1668–1774) wrote about human "knowing" involving an "imaginary construction of order in experience" (Mahoney, 2005: 747). Immanuel Kant (1724–1804), who is sometimes considered to be the first to have put forward constructivist ideas, described the mind as "an active organ which transforms the chaos of experience into orderly thought" (ibid.). It is worth pausing here briefly, as the history of constructivism is considered, since Kant is thought to have influenced Jean Piaget, a more well-known twentieth-century psychologist. Piaget is best known for the development of his theory of genetic epistemology, which we will consider later. Piaget's thoughts on constructivist learning seem to have been based on some of the ideas first promulgated by Kant. This is not the place to delve into the detail of Kant's work, except to say that his three "Critiques" (1781, 1788 and 1790) contain many ideas which were later nurtured and have grown, along with the thoughts of more recent constructivist thinkers, into a part of the wider constructivist school of thought.

Vaihinger (1852–1933) elaborated on some of Kant's ideas. In his philosophy "As If", published in 1911, Vaihinger argued that the purpose of the mind and of mental processes is not to reflect reality, but to assist individuals on their journeys through the multifarious circumstances of life. This implies that mental effort is directed towards making sense of what is experienced on the journey of life and constructing an understanding of the many varied experiences encountered on the way.

George Kelly (1963), writing of his radical rethinking of the ways that we construct our understanding of our experiences, was influenced by Vaihinger's work. Kelly suggests that we live in two fundamental worlds. The first world exists outside of any human understanding; the second is the world based upon the ways in which we interpret the primary world, which is an individual enterprise, in the form of representations or constructs. Kelly's work has been claimed as an intellectual source and inspiration by more writers in what are sometimes seen as mutually exclusive schools of thought than any other writer. He claims surprise at the fact that his work is even considered as a part of the wider cognitive canon.

Constructivism, considered in its widest sense, is concerned with more than a theory of learning. First, and perhaps most importantly within the context of this book, is the notion of constructivist epistemology. Epistemology is a consideration and detailed study of knowledge. Epistemologists seek to investigate and understand the origin, nature, methods and limits of human knowledge. Constructivist epistemology is a philosophical approach to investigating the scope, structure and very nature of knowledge which follows a constructivist approach. Constructivist epistemology is a philosophical perspective taken by some philosophers towards the nature of scientific knowledge. Constructivist epistemologists consider that scientific knowledge is constructed by scientists and not discovered from the world. This rather complex idea will become clearer as this book unfolds and the nature of constructivist learning is explored.

Constructivism is also a major area for concern in international relations, in mathematics (especially in the field of constructing mathematical proof) and in art and architecture (a strong constructivist movement developed in Russia at the beginning of the twentieth century). The proponents of constructivism in art rejected the idea of what was known as "art for art's sake". In its place, they worked towards art being an enterprise directed towards social purposes and social change. Constructivism in art and architecture lasted only into the 1930s, but it seems to have had a noticeable effect on developments in art in the developing new order in Germany and elsewhere at that time. There is a branch of psychology which is not concerned with learning, which is also a part of the wider constructivist movement. Constructivism in this context is concerned with an approach to psychological research and therapy. There is also a constructivist branch of linguistics in which the acquisition of language is studied from a constructivist perspective.

However, for our purposes, constructivism as a theory of learning and social constructivism as a development and subset of constructivist learning theory which considers and develops a theory about the social nature of learning are the crucial areas for investigation.

The beginnings of constructivist learning theory

We have seen that the notion of constructivist theory might actually date back to Greek times with Heraclitus seen as the earliest Western contributor. It is possible to look to Buddha and Lao Tzu for even earlier, partial references to the ideas encompassed by the philosophy. However, for our purposes, and in more focused consideration of learning in particular, we can place the real development of constructivist learning theory in the twentieth century.

Early twentieth-century attempts at regularising an approach to understanding how learning takes place were centred on what have become known as behaviourist or, sometimes, stimulus–response theories. The notable scientists who developed this school of learning theory are: Pavlov (1849–1936) for the development of classical conditioning at the beginning of the twentieth century; Watson (1878–1958) for setting out the initial principles of behaviourism; and Skinner (1904–1990) for his pioneering work on the importance of reinforcement. Behaviourism has been largely set aside as theory of learning with importance for schools and other formal contexts. However, in many training situations for specific functions where an automatic response might be needed, a behaviourist regime can be an effective approach. There are also a small number of occasions in a school setting when an automatic response, which can often take place with little or no understanding, is acceptable. An example of this might be in the realm of safety in a PE lesson. When a teacher asks, in a regularised way, for everyone to stop what they are doing, it might be very important that this happens immediately and without question. A signal such as a blast on a whistle might be introduced to the class trained to respond appropriately. In a more academic way, the response to a simple multiplication might be needed on a regular basis in order for a child to make progress with some other aspect of their learning in maths. Some teachers encourage the ability to make rapid responses to quick-fire multiplication questions with this in mind. Teachers recognise that the answers may well be returned in an automatic way and that the child can make the correct response. The teacher will also recognise that a full and detailed understanding of the notion of multiplication and the multiplication fact in question may not be present. Teachers strive for pupils attaining understanding, but as an introductory stage this behaviouristic response will satisfy the teacher and, in a perfect world, will precede more work which will encourage understanding. Despite this being an interesting area to consider, this book is not the place to dwell on this aspect of learning.

Within the realm of learning theory, the constructivist movement probably has the most understandable title. As the name suggests, the theory draws a picture of knowledge and understanding being slowly constructed. The building metaphor continues, as we will see, with the use of other terms, such as "scaffolding", which are used to illustrate the nature of the progress of learning and the support systems which may enhance the process. However, it is more than a general building of knowledge and understanding that is put forward; the constructivist model of learning suggests that constructive learning is an individual matter. Each of us will build an idiosyncratic version of reality based partly on identical experiences but shaped by individual experience and, importantly, upon an individual's prior knowledge, understanding and experience. That means that two learners exposed to exactly the same learning experience (e.g. a planned lesson) are likely to have different learning outcomes as a result of, amongst other things, what they already knew about the subject and how they interpret the items of knowledge presented to them and how they undertake the activities during the lesson. We will come back to this concept in more detail in later chapters.

As we have seen, the constructivist movement is a wider vision of life and society. It is much more than a vehicle for describing the processes involved in learning. The beginning of the constructivist approach to learning is considered to be the work of Jean Piaget (1896–1980). Piaget, who worked in the mid- and late twentieth century, was not a social constructivist. However, his work led to the expansion of understanding of child development and learning as a process of construction that has underpinned much of the theory relating to social constructivism. This may seem slightly at odds with the dates of one of the most important early social constructivists since Lev Vygotsky (1896–1934), working in a secretive Russia at the beginning of the twentieth century, in some cases predates Piaget. They worked in parallel with similar but occasionally diverging ideas.

In 1962 Piaget wrote of his failure to have met Vygotsky:

> It is not without sadness that an author discovers, twenty-five years after its publication, the work of a colleague who has died in the meantime, when that work contains so many points of immediate interest to him which should have been discussed personally and in detail. Although my friend A. Luria kept me up to date concerning Vygotsky's sympathetic and yet critical position with respect to my work, I was never able to read his writings or to meet him in person, and in reading his book today, I regret this profoundly, for we could have come to an understanding on a number of points.
>
> (Piaget, 1962: 1)

Piaget wrote these comments after reading in manuscript Chapter 2 and excerpts from Chapter 6 of Vygotsky's *Thought and Language*.

Apart from his stage developmental theory, which sets out four separate stages in the intellectual development of children and adolescents (sensori-motor, pre-operational, concrete operational and formal operations), Piaget is well known for describing the two main processes by which individuals deal with new information and sensory data and use this to build new knowledge and understanding.

An overview of the social constructivist approach to theory

We have seen that within the field of social constructivism there is great emphasis laid upon the importance of social context. We are told that there are two aspects of social context which affect the progress and extent of learning (Gredler, 1997; Wertsch, 1991): first, the systems garnered by the learner from his or her particular culture, such as language, the use of mathematical systems and logic, which develop throughout life; second, social interaction with more knowledgeable members of the community. Social interaction with more knowledgeable others is necessary if younger learners are to acquire, internalise and understand the meaning of the symbol systems (particularly language) in use in the community and to become capable of using them effectively. Thinking skills develop in children as they interact with those around them, especially adults.

Social constructivist theory emphasises the importance of culture and context in understanding what is experienced in the wider community and in constructing knowledge built on this understanding (Derry, 1999; McMahon, 1997). The importance of culture and context is highlighted in the theories of Vygotsky, Bruner, Bandura and others.

We will first consider three aspects of social constructivist thinking, namely: reality, knowledge and learning.

- *Reality*: Social constructivists tell us that reality is constructed through shared human social activity. Members of a community create the properties of the world which they share and which they understand in an agreed way (Kukla, 2000). Reality is not an entity waiting to be discovered; it is seen by social constructivists as something to be made by the individual. Reality is not something which can already exist in the form arrived at by one individual because each individual will construct their own reality which will not necessarily coincide with the reality of others. In practice, our individual realities will be very similar, but there are cases where, as a result of different fundamental experiences and interactions, they can be very different.

- *Knowledge*: Social constructivists also tell us that knowledge is a human creation and that it is constructed by social and cultural means (Ernest, 1999; Gredler, 1997; Prawat and Floden, 1994). Meaning and understanding are created by individuals by means of their social interactions and their interaction with their environment. In the same way as realities can vary, the knowledge held by some can be different from that held by others. Sometimes this is a question of completeness, at other times it can be a question of misconstruction based on the individual interpretation of experience and interaction, which in turn interacts with the individual's pre-existing knowledge.

- *Learning*: Social constructivists tell us that learning is a social process. It is neither simply an individual process, nor a passive process (McMahon, 1997; Pritchard, 2009). Effective and lasting learning takes place for the individual when engaged in social activity with a range of others, when in a social context and when new or repeated sensory input (e.g. words, pictures, music, stories and much more) is related to pre-existing knowledge and understanding.

Constructivist learning theory: This theory is based on the central notion that as learners we construct our own understanding of the world around us based on experience as we live and grow. We select and transform information from past and current knowledge and experience into new personal knowledge and understanding.

Social constructivist learning theory: This theory is a subtheory – though it is also important in its own right – which emphasises the role of others and all forms of social interaction in the process of constructing knowledge and understanding.

Social learning theory: This theory emphasises the role of observation and participation as a means of learning. It does not rule out interaction with others, but this interaction is stressed less than in social constructivism. Social interaction plays a fundamental role in the development of cognition.

Behaviourism: This theory is an early description of the ways in which learning takes place and, importantly in this context, behaviour is modified. There are times when a behaviourist approach is of value. It is important in training situations where precision of action and efficiency of effort are called for (e.g. pilot training) and it can be useful to apply behaviourist strategies in the management of children's behaviour and learning in classrooms.

Social constructivist ideas and some of their early proponents

Constructivist ideas can be seen as being divided into two distinctive camps. The first, which is encapsulated by von Glasersfeld's radical constructivism, is centred on the idea that each individual constructs reality for him or herself. Von Glasersfeld proposes two main claims:

(a) knowledge is not passively received but actively built up by the cognizing subject;

(b) the function of cognition is adaptive and serves the organization of the experiential world, not the discovery of ontological reality.

(von Glasersfeld 1989: 162)

In other words, all experience is subjective and filtered through a net, or a set of nets, of individual perception, bias and other sensory experience. The mind receives and then organises everything into what is then considered to be reality.

Von Glasersfeld's radical constructivism is seen by some as an opposing version of constructivism to the whole area of social constructivism. For this reason, and before we delve into social constructivism, we will consider this opposing element of constructivist learning theory. As in many theoretical arenas, there are complementary and sometimes competing camps within camps. Put crudely, constructivist learning theorists are divided between the so-called "radicals" and "socials". Both radical constructivists and social constructivists assert that objective reality is not perceived directly and that we construct our view of the world based on sensory input of all kinds and the interaction of this input with pre-existing knowledge. Radical constructivists believe that we develop our individual view of the world alone. Social constructivists, however, believe that we only build knowledge of our surroundings through discourse with others, that is, through social interaction.

Social constructivism really emphasises the role of culture and context in developing personal and shared interpretations and understanding of reality. Social constructivism has emerged, for the most part, from the work of Piaget, Vygotsky, Bruner and Bandura. The faction of constructivism which emphasises the social elements of learning and experience shares at least one major point of foundation with radical constructivism: the idea that reality is constructed by the individual. But for social constructivists this constructed product cannot come into being before its social invention. That is, knowledge is a social product, and learning is a social process. Meaning and understanding is forged out of an agreement between social partners which is honed by social interaction assisted by the essential medium and assumptions of language.

Vygotsky's notion of the ZPD (see Figure 1.1) is a crucial precept which is central to all of social constructivist learning theory. The ZPD describes the difference between what a person can learn on his or her own and what that person can learn when learning is supported by a more knowledgeable other. Appropriate and timely interventions in the course of learning within an individual's ZPD has become an essential strategy for teachers working with the social constructivist approach. Vygotsky's social constructivism, and the concept of a ZPD in particular, will be dealt with in detail later.

Piaget's genetic epistemology

The title of this area of developmental psychology comes from its origins in Piaget's background and interest in biology and the growth of organisms. It refers to the birth and growth ("genesis") of knowledge (broadly, "epistemology", more specifically, epistemology is the study or theory of knowledge). Genetic epistemology looks at the validity of an individual's constructed knowledge in relation to the process of its construction. Genetic epistemology considers the soundness of resultant knowledge according to the process undertaken to establish it.

Piaget's work on the development of knowledge and understanding is founded upon the basic view that there is a set of processes which are unconsciously put into action each time an individual encounters information from any of their senses. In practice, this means all of the time. To explain the processes, it is easiest to isolate occasions when sensory information is encountered and outline the possible mental processes that are initiated and followed through.

Piaget describes three essential processes which define the basis of the way in which, according to the theory of genetic epistemology, learning takes place. These are: assimilation, accommodation and equilibration. Before defining these processes, we will look at the notion of schemas, which is an integral element of Piaget's theory.

Schemas: All living, thinking beings have a set of rules which are variously known as "scripts", "schemes" and, as we will be using, "schemas" that are used to interpret their everyday surroundings. Schemas are integrated

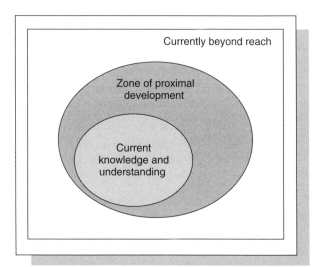

Figure 1.1 Zone of proximal development (ZPD)

networks of knowledge which are stored in long-term memory and allow us to recall, understand and create expectations. This allows us to operate in a world that becomes increasingly familiar and understandable with the passage of time as the schemas are built up and increasingly interlinked.

A schema is a representational model of all of the knowledge that an individual has of any given topic. Schemas are organised around themes or topics; the individual elements of a schema are linked by this common theme. At a simple level, all that a young child knows about cars might be that they travel from place to place, it is necessary to drive one, they are red, they have a distinct smell, there is a seat for a child in the back and luggage can be carried in the boot. On every occasion that the child experiences anything concerning a car – a horn, a different colour, a screeching sound from the brakes – this new information will be added to the fast-growing schema for the car. The car schema will have many links to other schemas based upon what other topics have in common with cars – there may well be a lorry schema, a bus schema, a red schema and so on. Our schemas are very large and constantly growing and there are a great many links both within and between our schemas. It is actually quite a difficult situation to understand and this is probably because it is actually a model which, although useful at a rudimentary level, is deficient in some ways, such as when trying to model extremely complex actions or the multitudinous connections which exist in highly complex areas of our lives.

When new information is processed it is considered by the extent to which it fits into an existing schema. In many cases it is possible that new information does not fit well into an existing schema. This is because the individual has little or no pre-existing knowledge which relates to or sheds light on the nature of meaning of the new incoming information. This is when we are puzzled or surprised by something which we experience – we cannot easily relate it to something which we "know" already. In these cases, we have to either add the new information to an existing schema or alter a schema to allow for the new evidence which has been received. We have to assimilate or accommodate in order to maintain a state of equilibrium, that is, a state within which we are not attempting to deal with contradictions. On some occasions a denial may be made, for example, "That can't be a car because it only has three wheels."

Bartlett (1886–1969) (see Eysenck, 2004) carried out extensive work and wrote widely on the subject of schemas. One example of the work that he did and which throws light on the nature of schemas related to remembering stories. He argued that we rely on schemas to remember stories. These claims were based upon his findings of experimental subjects recalling a story from a different culture. The nature of the errors made by the subjects of the experiment, in Bartlett's interpretation, underlines the ways in which schemas work and the importance of prior knowledge, held in schemas, for developing new understanding. The types of errors made were rationalisation, flattening and sharpening. Altering the story to read like a more typical story from their own culture was the most common error, a rationalisation error. A flattening error was the failure to recall details which were not familiar to them. The sharpening errors were elaboration of certain details which were more familiar to them. The subjects reconstructed the details according to their expectations of "what must have happened", which is according to their own personal structure of schemas (Bransford, 1979: 159). They made the new information match their existing schemas. Bartlett reported this in 1932. Bartlett used the results to exemplify the nature of schemas and their role in understanding and recall. The subjects of the experiment were attempting to relate information from a culture alien to them to schemas which were rooted firmly in their own (English) culture (Bartlett in Anderson, 1990).

Assimilation, accommodation and equilibration

Assimilation: In Piagetian terms, assimilation is the collecting and classifying of new information. As we have seen, a schema is a notional representation of what an individual knows (or can do) and consists of discrete items of knowledge which are linked to each other by the common theme of the schema. When new information is encountered – a car with no roof, a car painted with flowers – this is added to the existing schema. It is assimilated. However, it will only be assimilated if it does not contradict something already established as an integral part of what exists. If it seems that the new information is actually plausible or if it presents itself on many occasions despite the apparent contradiction – "I didn't know that a car could have a trailer attached" – the schema is added to and the information is assimilated. This process is linked very closely to accommodation.

Accommodation: This is the alteration of a schema in order for new and contradictory information to be allowed. The above example of a car with three wheels can be used to illustrate this. A child happily recognises that the car-shaped vehicle with four wheels and other more usual features is a car. Each time one is seen, the word "car" is spoken and some positive feedback might be given, "Yes, that's a car." When a less common car, a three-wheeled model from the past, is experienced for the first time, it is very likely that the very young child will not be able to relate this to his current understanding of what a car is. The child might have the car pointed out and not recognise that this new version is actually a car. There will perhaps be a time of denial. This will be followed by a period of adjustment, possibly over some time, and eventually, based on experience, the three-wheeled car will be admitted to the car schema and links will be made to other schemas, such as the bike/trike schema, and a situation of no contradiction will be returned to. As living, thinking beings we strive for a situation of no contradiction. In this sense, we strive for equilibrium.

Equilibration: This is the state of having no contradictions present in our mental representations of our environment. The linked processes of assimilation and accommodation are the means by which a state of equilibrium is sought. Equilibration is said to follow a threefold path. First, we are satisfied with our mode of thought and said to be in a state of equilibrium. Second, if we become aware of a shortcoming or contradiction in our existing thinking we become dissatisfied and enter a state of disequilibrium; we experience cognitive conflict. Third, we move to a more sophisticated mode of thought. We are able to eliminate the contradiction of the previous mode and in that way regain equilibrium; the cognitive conflict has been dealt with. We can all usually remember examples of situations similar to the ones above, some in our early childhood, others from later in life.

Schemas can be used not only to interpret but also to make predictions. Consider a situation where you were able to understand what was said by another person even though what they said did not necessarily make complete sense. If you were asked to pass the "what's it", it is very likely in a given situation that you would know what was meant. You would be able to predict what is meant and correctly interpret "what's it" as the spanner needed to tighten the neck of the waste pipe leading from beneath the sink where the person asking for the "what's it" is working. Information that does not fit into a schema is most likely to not be understood or not be understood correctly. This is the reason why a reader might have a difficult time understanding a text on a subject they are not familiar with, even if they recognise and understand the meaning of the individual words in the passage.

Piaget's genetic epistemology also explains the process of how a human being develops intellectually from birth throughout life. As we briefly considered earlier, four stages of development – sensorimotor (birth to two years), preoperational (two to seven years), concrete operational (seven to eleven years) and formal operational (eleven years and up) – are described and children's intellectual growth is measured against them. This set of stages made a great impact on educational practice during the 1950s and 1960s. However, it has, to a large extent, been left behind and become a far less important aspect of Piaget's work. New research has shown that precise and discreet developmental stages are not nearly as simple to describe, nor are they as rigidly linear as Piaget, on the surface at least, seems to suggest. (See Donaldson 1978.)

Vygotsky's social learning

Lev Vygotsky, a Russian psychologist working in the early twentieth century, only became known in the West many years after his seminal works were published in his homeland. The secrecy of the USSR meant that his writing was neither translated nor made available for many years. However, his theory of social development, particularly his work on learning in social contexts, has become central to current thinking and practice in education.

Vygotsky considers that social interaction is a fundamental aspect of successful cognitive and intellectual growth. Vygotsky places great emphasis on dialogue and other interaction between the learner and an other. He tells us that

> [e]very function in the child's cultural development appears twice: first, on the social level, and later, on the individual level; first, between people (interpsychological) and then inside the child (intrapsychological). This applies equally to voluntary attention, to logical memory, and to the formation of concepts. All the higher functions originate as actual relationships between individuals.
>
> (Vygotsky, 1978: 57)

Another crucially important element of Vygotsky's work is the idea that the potential for cognitive development and learning is dependent upon transition across the ZPD. This important aspect of Vygotsky's work can be explained simply. The ZPD is a notional area of understanding or cognitive development that is close to but just beyond a learner's current level of understanding. If learners are to make "progress" they must be helped to move into this zone and then beyond it to a new and higher level. From this new level there will of course be a new ZPD, implying a capacity for more development at every stage. In Vygotsky's own words, the ZPD is the

> level of potential development as determined through problem solving under adult guidance or in collaboration with more capable peers. . . What children can do with the assistance of others might be in some sense

even more indicative of their mental development than what they can do alone.

(Vygotsky, 1978)

Successful and timely movement across this notional zone is dependant upon social interaction. Learners can be assisted in the progress made across their ZPD in a given situation by a more knowledgeable other who can provide the sort of support that will make progress possible. In a sense, measured social interaction is a tool for allowing progress to be made. We will look in more detail at the nature of this support, known as "scaffolding", later in this book. Progress across a ZPD is central to learning and in the context of a social classroom it is usually, but not exclusively, the teacher who takes the role of scaffolder. In formal learning situations the role of scaffolder can be a complex part to play. The nature of scaffolding and the types of interventions that teachers can make will be looked at in more detail later. It is interesting to briefly note here that the scaffolder need not always be a teacher or even an adult. The term "more knowledgeable other" is used to suggest that social interaction with any other individual has the potential to support Vygotskian learning. This might be in the context of group or paired work in a classroom or it might be in the informal context of two friends chatting about a topic of interest in a park, at home or anywhere else for that matter.

Bruner's learning theory

Bruner worked extensively almost throughout the entire twentieth century and made a series of very important contributions to educational and psychological theory. We will not delve into the detail of his work here – there is far too much of it – but we will consider his view of learning as an active, social process. One of Bruner's major themes is that learning is an active process in which learners construct new ideas or concepts based upon their current and pre-existing knowledge. The learners select and transform information, construct hypotheses and make decisions with reference to and reliance upon an internal cognitive structure. This cognitive structure which he refers to is the network of schemas which provide meaning and structure to experience and allow the individual to build on what is already known in order to go further.

In terms of teaching, Bruner considers that the teacher should try to encourage pupils to discover principles for themselves; the teacher and pupil should engage in an active dialogue in order to meet this end. The role of the teacher is to help in the process of transforming whatever information is to be learned into a format which is appropriate to the learner's current state of understanding. Bruner was the first to state that a curriculum should be organised "spirally" so that the pupil continually revisits ideas and facts and is able to build upon what has been learned previously.

For Bruner, learning is an active, social process in which learners construct new ideas and concepts based on their current knowledge. Social contact with others – the teacher, in many formal learning contexts – is a key element of the process. The pupil, mostly unconsciously, selects the information, creates hypotheses and then integrates this new material into their existing knowledge and mental constructs – schemas. The medium of language has great importance for Bruner, as it has for other social constructivists (Bruner, 1983; Berliner, 1998).

Bandura's social cognitive theory

Bandura developed a social cognitive theory which in part paid homage to Piaget's earlier work. He considers learning to be an active process, in line with all constructivist thinking, and stresses the importance of the social nature of learning.

Bandura's major theoretical beliefs are fully consistent with social constructivist thought. He points out that human lives are not lived in isolation (Royer, 2004). He writes about what he terms "collective agency", which is an extension of more individualised "human agency". The notion of collective agency is concerned with people working together on shared beliefs and common aspirations to improve their lives. In *Self-efficacy: The Exercise of Control* (1997) Bandura describes his theory of self-efficacy and its application to education, health, psychopathology, athletics, business and international affairs.

Bandura argues that people learn from observing role models in day-to-day life. He explains that, "Learning would be exceedingly laborious, not to mention hazardous, if people had to rely solely on the effects of their own actions to inform them what to do" (1977: 22).

Situated learning

The notion of Bandura's observational learning links with yet another aspect of social constructivism. It links with the concept of situativity, which is encapsulated within the theory of situated learning (Lave and Wenger, 1991), which we will very briefly look at here. Situated learning and what is referred to as the "apprenticeship model" is a description of learning that takes place in highly social situations. In this sense, the word "social" refers to a situation in which two or more individuals are together and interacting in one or more of a variety of different ways, but specifically in a way that encourages learning to take place for one or more of the participants. The label "apprenticeship" is used as a reference to the master craftsman and young apprentice model of traditional learning in any of the craft or more physical occupations. The apprentice, in a way, looks and learns (cf. Bandura's observational learning). The apprentice is guided in his efforts to master a new skill by the highly skilled master. The way that learning proceeds is by demonstration and instruction, followed by attempts on the part of the apprentice to emulate the master, followed by a good deal of practice. It is considered that the apprentice, by sheer proximity to the master and by a level of social engagement, will acquire the skills in question. The notion of legitimate peripheral participation also comes out of this area of theory. In a social group, where it is expected that the younger members of the group will learn the skills and acquire the knowledge that is commonly held within the group, the learner is said to be a legitimate participant. The fact that the learner is not a central member of the group makes him a peripheral member, hence he is a legitimate peripheral participant. This notion of how some learning progresses can be seen in, for example, younger children learning the skills and rules of a game by joining in with older children who have the skills and understand the rules involved.

So, another important social constructivist notion is that of situated learning, which is sometimes referred to as or linked with the notion of authentic learning. It is where the learner undertakes activities which are directly relevant to the application of the learning in question and which take place within a culture which is familiar and in a similar context to those in which the learning might be applied in the future.

Genetic epistemology: This is a general theoretical framework developed by Jean Piaget. It is focused on the concept of cognitive structure. According to this concept, cognitive structures are patterns of physical or mental action which specify acts of intelligence and correspond to stages of child development.

Schema: A schema is a notional mental representation of the world or, more specifically, an aspect of the world. A schema is an individual's representation of a concept, an item of knowledge or an action that can be revised when new information is encountered by the individual.

Assimilation, accommodation and equilibration: Assimilation is the process by which schemas are reorganised and developed. New information can be assimilated as long as it does not contradict the existing schema. Schemas are altered and restructured when new alternate or contradictory information arises – this is accommodation. Equilibrium is a state of balance for a schema when there are no conflicting elements. Equilibrium is the state which is innately sought by individuals.

Zone of proximal development (ZPD): This is a central plank of Vygotsky's social constructivism. It refers to the notional area of knowledge and understanding that is just beyond what a learner has complete control over. With help, learners are able to move forward into this zone and achieve more than they could alone. Once a zone has been negotiated, a new zone, which is a little further ahead, still becomes apparent.

Interpsychological: This is Vygotsky's term for mental activity which is between people (i.e. on a social plane). This is the plane where thoughts and ideas are first formulated.

Intrapsychological: This is Vygotsky's term for mental activity which is wholly internal. This is an individual activity whereby ideas are internalised and better understood.

Situated learning: This is based on the concept that learning normally occurs as the function of an activity which is in a specific context and culture. Learning takes place in relation to place, time and cultural surroundings. It is often unintentional rather than deliberate.

Apprenticeship: In terms of learning theory, this term refers to the relationship between an expert and a novice. By observation and gradually increasing participation, the novice learns from the actions, words and possibly instruction and demonstration of the expert. This model does not necessarily imply a formal teaching and learning situation.

Summary

- The constructivist movement has a long history and has influenced many areas of human life.

- Constructivism, in terms of learning, considers that individuals construct their own understanding of the world around them by accumulating information and interpreting it in relation to previous experiences.

- Social constructivism embraces schools of thought that emphasise social contact, interaction and context.

- Social learning theorists describe the ways in which social interaction with those around us, no matter what the precise relationship might be, has a profound effect on our learning.

Activities

- Consider, in the light of the content of this chapter, the major differences between earlier attempts at describing the way that learners learn and the constructivist view of learning.

- Compare the different branches of constructivist theories.

2

Research

Evidence drawn from current, recent and past practice

By the end of this chapter you will be able to:

- identify sources of empirical evidence relating to the social classroom;
- identify approaches that are designed to support learning in a social classroom;
- identify the basis for the underpinning beliefs and the precepts with regard to social constructivist theories.

In this chapter, we will consider research in the area of the social classroom. Examples are drawn from the work of well-established psychologists and educationalists reflecting recent and current classroom practice. The five different sources of empirical evidence illustrate different approaches to research in the area; they will then connect with the theories in Chapter 3.

Before the emergence of social constructivism, many theories ignored an important facet of learning: the social dimension. Through the examples of empirical research, the key issues relating to social aspects of learning will be illustrated. The following examples of research focus on social interaction to enable learning and the exploitation of the social context to enhance learning.

In recent years, the pervasive nature of constructivist ideas has had and is having an influence upon research itself, particularly classroom-based research. The pervasive nature of social constructivist ideas is also influencing classroom practice. It is the purpose of this chapter to present empirical evidence to show how theory can be established, pedagogy can be rationalised and, eventually, teaching strategies can evolve.

Classroom success and social interaction

This example of empirical evidence comes from considering teachers' perceptions of their learners' social competence and the implications that has for learning. The research, by Megan Wight and Christine Chapparo, probes the relationship between learning and the skills of social interaction (Wight and Chapparo, 2008). They carried out a comparative study of two groups of pupils: one group was succeeding and the other was having difficulties in the classroom. They used a measure of social competence and determined that there is a correlation between social and learning competences and, importantly, that strategies to develop social competences would be beneficial to the pupils' learning. To measure learning and the social dimension they used a social competency grid, Skillstreaming (McGinnis and Goldstein, 1997), which included reference to those aspects of behaviour and abilities that are essential to classroom learning (teacher–learner instructional), those aspects that foster friendships (learner–learner) and the intrapersonal dealings with feelings, aggression and stress. The research provides the empirical evidence supporting the idea that classroom success is closely linked with the interpersonal skills of the learner and the way in which he or she interrelates with others, the extrapersonal skills of the pupil dealing with the external motivations of the teacher, classroom procedures and school-imposed policies and the interpersonal skills related to the emotional aspects of learning. It establishes the link between social interaction and learning. The study identified that the boys with learning difficulties were perceived by their teachers as having poorer social performance across multiple domains when compared to their typically developing peers. Implications of these findings are that children's social performance may negatively impact learning and classroom participation and that, for some children, social competence should be a focus of occupational therapy assessment and treatment.

This model of social interaction is centred on the individual pupil. He or she will have a two-way relationship with the teacher that may not necessarily separate out the communications made by the teacher to the child from those made by the teacher to the whole class. The level of social awareness of the pupil will be a determining factor relating to the learner's classroom success. The pupil will have many relationships with other individual pupils and will also have a perception of his or her place in the class as a whole. Again, the social awareness of the individual pupil will determine if he or she is aware of the differences. This model of classroom interaction helps us to interpret and therefore understand what is taking place in the classroom.

The Teacher Skillstreaming Checklist (Wight and Chapparo, 2008: 260) identifies five subscales of social skills which impact upon classroom success relating to:

- doing what is expected (described as "classroom survival skills");
- making friends;
- dealing with feelings;
- dealing with aggression;
- dealing with stress.

The checklist underpins a practical approach to ensuring pupils have the competences to succeed in a socially-orientated classroom.

For another example of empirical evidence gathering, it is the social and emotional aspects of learning (SEAL) to which we now turn.

Social and emotional aspects of learning (SEAL)

Social and emotional aspects of learning (SEAL) is a school initiative in England. It provides a framework for explicitly promoting social, emotional and behavioural aspects of learning. The intention is that this should lead to school improvement, for example, in behaviour, attendance and learning. These developments occur at a time when teaching strategies are refocusing upon the child with other initiatives such as Every Child Matters (ECM) in September 2003, ECM: Next Steps in March 2004 and the Children Act in 2004. The personalisation agenda initiated by Prime Minister Tony Blair in 2003 at the Labour Party conference stated "At secondary school, [there will be] personalised learning for every child" (Blair, 2003). The policy continues to be supported by successive ministers in a range of public sector areas (DCSF, 2009a), the National Strategy (DfES, 2005a, b) and the Byron Report (DCSF, 2008). The motivation is driven by the general acceptance that unsuccessful adults arise from unsuccessful children. The idea that patterns of antisocial behaviour in schools are predictors of antisocial behaviour in adult life is supported by research (Farrington, 1988; Robins,

1986). The observation that nearly all antisocial adults have previously shown poor behaviour as children (Robins, 1986) motivates the political will to empower public services, particularly education, to promote social and emotional well-being of children and young people.

This section describes research in the area of social and emotional development and its importance within the social classroom. The underpinning empirical evidence arises through the study of studies, which is also called "meta-analysis". Contrasting analyses will be used to illustrate the point that empirical evidence can be drawn from studying other works. The first example is based in America and conducted by the Collaborative for Academic, Social, and Emotional Learning (CASEL) and carried out in conjunction with The National Center for Mental Health Promotion and Youth Violence Prevention. It draws empirical evidence from the systematic review of current literature reflecting recent thinking and trends. In this meta-analysis, researchers used statistical techniques to identify key factors in a large number of papers and reports of interventions. They then estimated the average reported impact across the reports. In this case there were 207 projects that involved 288,000 pupils. This mass study of the academic literature to draw overviews of the data is an important step between observation of classroom practice and the development of a theoretical construct and the further development of policy and principles of practice. The analysis revealed the following successful practices:

9% decrease in conduct problems, such as classroom misbehavior and aggression . . . 10% decrease in emotional distress, such as anxiety and depression . . . 9% improvement in attitudes about self, others, and school . . . 23% improvement in social and emotional skills . . . 9% improvement in school and classroom behaviour . . . 11% improvement in achievement test scores

(CASEL, 2008: 2)

Examples of good practice identified by the research include:

■ Successful strategies ensure pupils recognise and manage emotions, behave ethically and responsibly by caring about others and so develop positive relationships. They recognise that success in school leads to success in life. Those who do not possess these skills are less likely to succeed.

■ Successful social and emotional education programmes recognise the importance to pupils and others of the assessment processes and the impact they have upon the pupils' well-being. The CASEL study reflects in the era of "No Child Left Behind" (U.S. Department of Education, 2002)

following "A Nation At Risk: The Imperative For Educational Reform" and the National Commission on Excellence in Education (1983) with the implementation of high-stakes tests to establish accountability through open reporting of school, district and state results. The perception that positive child well-being is measured by national test results (Brown, 2008: 106) was still pervasive at the time of the CASEL (2008) study.

■ Good practices in social and emotional learning show variation, flexibility, differentiation and inclusion. Most importantly, the promotion of social and emotional learning goals is not seen as being separate or even parallel to the academic policy of schools. It is taught alongside and within traditional subjects. Those initiatives that are effective are provided within supportive environments and foster a climate that is caring, safe, supportive and conducive to success.

These findings are compelling evidence to warrant the classroom interventions that will be described in later chapters of this book. The CASEL study identifies four characteristics of the successful programmes and uses the acronym SAFE – sequenced, active, focused and explicit. Those programmes

> [u]se a Sequenced set of activities to develop SE [social and emotional] skills in a step-by-step fashion; Use Active forms of learning, such as role-plays and behavioral rehearsal that provide students with opportunities to practice SE skills; Focus attention on SEL [social and emotional learning], with at least eight sessions devoted to SE skill development; and Explicitly target particular SE skills for development, with skills identified in lessons' learning objectives.
>
> (CASEL, 2008: 2–3)

The empirical basis for linking social and emotional learning to school success comes from a growing body of knowledge (Adi *et al.*, 2007; Goleman, 1996; National Commission on Excellence in Education, 2008; Weare and Gray, 2003; Wells *et al.*, 2002; Zins *et al.*, 2004). Joseph Zins and his colleagues identify that schools will be most successful in their educational pursuit when they bring together pupils' academic, social and emotional learning and do not separate the academic/subject learning from the pastoral aspects of the curriculum. It is more generally accepted that social and emotional well-being is important to the overall success of the pupil in school in terms of the nonacademic outcomes. However, their studies conclude that social and emotional learning has a role in improving pupils' academic performance and lifelong learning. Their evidence links school attitudes, behaviour and performance (Zins *et al.*, 2004). In the review of 80 nationally available programmes in the United States in 2003, they found that about a third of them promoted integration by including direct connections between the teaching and learning of the subjects and social and emotional learning. Examples described include applying social and emotional strategies when setting study goals: "83% of the programs produced academic gains. In addition, 12% of the programs that did not specifically target academic performance documented an impact on academic achievement" (Zins *et al.*, 2004: 14).

A UK-based study of studies based on the work of Katherine Weare and Gay Gray at the University of Southampton (Weare and Gray, 2003) established the supporting evidence for the introduction of a UK-wide initiative in social and emotional education. That evidence is drawn from the evaluation of programmes and initiatives that aim to increase pupils' social and emotional learning and well-being. It focuses upon the teaching of the skills, attitudes and behaviour relating to social and emotional learning, but it draws from a wide range of sources including out-of-school, in-class, whole-school and individualised support.

Aristotle first encapsulated the term "holism" in the phrase "the whole is greater than the sum of the parts". The underlying principle of this survey of practice is to identify the holistic nature of the provision for social and emotional aspects of learning. The research focused upon the measurable impact of these whole-school, contextual, environmental, cross-curriculum, integrated approaches. In contrast to the previously described study of classroom impacts, this study focused upon policy and the local authority aspect of implementation. As a consequence, the evidence obtained supports holistic approaches that change the emphasis from the behaviour of individual pupils to the actions of the teachers and other staff and the policies and procedures of the classroom and school, thus encouraging people, especially teachers and others working directly with children, to look at pupils in a holistic way. The researchers noted that a good deal of previous work on emotional and social competence has been for troubled and troublesome pupils. The five local authorities involved in this study identified the importance of the context and that the needs of the troubled minority are best met through providing a whole solution for the classroom or school. The survey identifies other principles arising from the empirical evidence and review of the literature. The most positive evidence of effectiveness arose when programmes:

- adopted a whole-school approach;
- included working with everyone, avoiding stigmatising the few;

- started early, were clear about expectations and boundaries and built warm relationships;
- supported teachers in the process;
- were aimed at the promotion of the positive as opposed to the prevention of the negative;
- were environmental and not simply curriculum-focused;
- were holistic, creating long-term impacts (i.e. changes to pupils' attitudes);
- were implemented continuously for more than a year.

These points are of value to those planning the introduction or development of personal and social elements of the curriculum.

The study also identified the fact that emotional, behavioural and social problems are widespread. They conclude "targeting [individuals] alone is not appropriate where there is a continuous or unimodal distribution of a problem" (Weare and Gray, 2003: 43).

Finally, they conclude the importance of the complementary nature of the two approaches: the environmental/holistic approach of working with all pupils and the approach of supporting specific children. They cite the work of Birmingham Local Authority as an example of this integration of support for social and emotional aspects of learning (Weare and Gray, 2003: 43–44).

Cooperation and collaboration in the classroom

Cooperation and collaboration in the classroom are distinctly different phenomena, but they are inextricably connected. Cooperation is a positive relationship between pupils that is characterised by support and helpfulness. In this discussion of the evidence supporting cooperation and collaboration in the classroom there will be a consideration of a number of concepts, including competition and motivation, cooperative and competitive activity, self-selected and assigned grouping, roles and responsibilities, peer teaching and peer tutoring, risk taking and trust and mastery and performance outcomes.

Aspects of cooperation and cooperative activity can be classified as cognitive or physical. The cognitive cooperative activities are where one learner helps the other learner to learn. These helping activities include doing (skills), showing (skills), telling (knowledge) and explaining (understanding). The physical sharing activities include loaning, giving, hiring (i.e. loaning for a return) and taking turns.

In cooperative activities, the learner retains autonomy; their learning goals are not determined by or impacted upon by other learners. Observation of cooperative learning includes the characteristic of the absence of clearly defined outcomes, activities, structures and planning. The interactions are informal, short-lived and of low intensity. Research by Winer and Ray (1994) has led to a number of representations of the relationship between co-operative working and collaboration:

> Collaboration is a process that gets people working together in new ways. The process does not end but spawns new collaborative ventures. Collaboration becomes a continuing phenomenon with a wide range of results that empower people and systems to change.
>
> (Winer and Ray, 1994: ix)

The heart of collaboration is the single goal being pursued by two or more learners. Collaboration can lead to a single product that is owned by all the participants. Collaboration is associated with group work, but not all group work is collaborative (Elliott, 2001). These ideas will be explored and related to strategies for teaching in Chapter 5. Observation shows that collaboration is more long-term and has a higher level of intensity than cooperation. The activities require commitment of time, responsibility and trust. They have clearly defined structures, plans, responsibilities (including leadership and other role types), activities and outcomes. There is a degree of risk taking by the individuals and, probably most importantly, collab-oration leads to learning. Here, the learning has the same goal driving it, but of course what is learned is unique to the individual. The idea of pro-moting collaborative learning is based upon the social constructivist rationale that learning and understanding is a socially constructed concept: "The key skill of working with others includes the ability to contribute to small-group and whole-class discussion, and to work with others to meet a challenge" (QCA, 1999: 22).

The interdependence of collaboration and cooperation can be summar-ised as follows: without cooperation no collaboration can take place; the expectation of collaboration fosters cooperation.

A recent survey of literature (Roseth et al., 2008) reflects the growing interest in establishing a better understanding of the social–cognitive factors of the classroom. It acknowledges that it is a minority (17 of 148) of empirical studies (Roseth et al., 2008: 239) that both measure academic impact and social impact of interactive classroom processes. However, it does identify the significance of the impact of social strategies on academic achievement. The studies focus upon cooperative, competitive and individualistic goal structures of adolescent education. The results indicate that with younger adolescent pupils, more positive peer relationships and higher academic achievement are associated with cooperative rather than competitive or individualistic goal structures. This has important implications for the planning of the curriculum and the activities that support learning.

The computer-based social learning environment

The next examples of empirical evidence for supporting the value of dialogue in learning environments come from computer-based examples. The advent of the new technologies in schools has introduced new words into the pedagogic language. This section will discuss the following keywords and phrases: "social networking and social cohesion", "identity switching and role experimentation", "lurking and anonymity", "authentic and simulated" and "synchronous and recorded".

The first example shows that quality peer discussions can arise from authentic, technology-mediated learning in science. Matthew Kearney's (2004) study focuses on the use of multimedia-based tasks with secondary school-age pupils. The tasks are designed to encourage the pupils to participate in discussion of science and their understanding of it. They are based on the predict-observe-explain format that is a pedagogically strong way to encourage scientific thinking and discussion. The pupils are encouraged to reveal and defend their own scientific beliefs and to challenge the beliefs of others. This is an interpretive approach where the researchers studied the pupil interactions using discourse analysis of audio and video recordings taken when small groups of pupils were around the computer discussing multimedia presentations. The authenticity of the learners' experiences arises from the fidelity of the simulated science-focused activity – the quality of the multimedia application to represent the salient aspects of the "real" experience. There is sufficient detail to inform the learner of the situation and the scientific processes.

The study adopts a social constructivist perspective to analyse and interpret the pupils' "articulation and justification of their science conceptions, clarification of and critical reflection on their partners' views, and negotiation of new, shared meanings" (Kearney, 2004: 427). The findings indicate that the computer-based tasks can stimulate discussion and encourage peer-learning conversations. In particular, the discussions are encouraged because of the prediction, reasoning and observational nature of the activity. The researcher also identifies that the increased level of pupil control of the learning tasks helps initiate quality peer discussions. However, the assertions are tempered by the observation that "students generally did not conduct rich conversations during the explanation stage of the POE [predict, observe and explain] tasks in this study" (Kearney, 2004: 448). This is explained by pupils' reluctance to admit to incorrect predictions and the fact that the pupils were more familiar with teacher-led and teacher-supported tasks. It is noted that the teacher role is particularly important when negotiating and interceding with differences of opinion. The study raises important questions about the role of the teacher in the social constructivist classroom. We will see again later that the role of the teacher/instructor, in the social classroom, is critical.

Arja Veerman (2003) reports on three studies where computer-mediated communication (CMC) is the media for dialogue between pupils in groups. One study uses a synchronous chat environment, Microsoft NetMeeting. Synchronous CMC is where the sender and recipient are online together and responses are immediate. Asynchronous systems, such as email, require the sender to wait, perhaps for hours or days, for a response. Synchronous communication is afforded by the more popular internet messenger systems such as Yahoo Talk, Microsoft Messenger and chat elements in Bebo and Facebook. The pupils discuss, in real-time, issues by making statements and responding to the statements of others. It is an environment that is familiar to many. (It will feature in a case study in Chapter 5.) The history of the pupils' dialogue is recorded and visible, therefore sustained discussion is afforded. In Veerman's study, she gave the learners clear tasks and foci for discussion. They were also given curriculum time (45–60 minutes) in which to carry out the chat sessions. There was an expectation upon the students that they would participate. To enhance the quality of dialogue, some students were also briefed upon different forms of peer coaching. The study illustrates, through empirical evidence, one of many scenarios using computer-based technologies that can successfully facilitate dialogue and constructive argument.

A study carried out by Catherine Richards (2009) focused upon the dialogues between students when discussing themes in a bounded chat environment. The empirical evidence from the research shows the efficacy of dialogue in a particular aspect of learning: emotional intelligence. She writes:

> Chat is able to offer relative equality of status so this makes it attractive. Social differences including those relating to gender or status are reduced and therefore, there is "status equalization" online. These differences are

not completely eradicated as clues to identity, for example through language, may be apparent. Females, for example, are shown to be chattier online and therefore, may sub-consciously give clues to their gender without realising. The immediacy of chat makes it very attractive to learners and chat is able to build on the increasing expectations that teachers and students have of e-learning and support. Chat, through positive interaction between student and teacher, can increase the social presence felt between the two parties and thus potentially increase class motivation. The research shows that male students and those at lower levels are more likely to access chat, therefore appearing more attracted to it but less likely to consider the full implications of their actions within it. This demonstrates that students are interested in using online mechanisms such as chat. Student interest is a critical driver for the introduction of chat in colleges and has been clearly demonstrated in the research. It is particularly suitable for students who may not access emotional literacy and pastoral care support in any other way and the research appears to show that these types of students are more likely to participate or "lurk" within such a system.

(Richards, 2009: 34)

This extract of the study touches upon important concepts and affordances associated with online classroom environments. The anonymity associated with the environment gives an equality of status and can overcome social structures of the open classroom and the difficulties that classrooms can sometimes present for individuals. Those difficulties might mean some individuals contribute poorly or do not contribute at all. The relationship between individual learners and the teacher is enriched through this extra dimension to their communication; this can lead to more positive relationships. The exchange of views and information between learners can lead to a greater social cohesion because, in general, in the online world the differences of opinion do not lead to conflict and breakdowns in relationship that are not retractable.

The anonymity of some chat environments can accommodate role experimentation and identity switching. Learners can experience people's reaction to the adopted roles. They can also learn from the attempt to articulate ideas from another person's perspective. This may include acting out fantasy situations or issues. It can offer the opportunity to feel empathy from others, although there needs to be acknowledgement of "cyber one-upmanship" (Adamse and Motta, 2000: 30).

An aspect of chat room behaviour is lurking (Mann and Stewart, 2000; Nonnecke and Preece, 1999; Marvin, 1995). Lurking is being present in a chat room and listening to or watching the conversations but not actively participating. From the study of an anonymised chat room (Richards, 2009), rates of lurking can be associated with different sorts of participants. For example, "some level 1 students made very minimal contributions so in reality they were acting as a type of lurker, for example, only adding [a phatic comment like] hi or an emoticon" (104). In the physical classroom, these phatic utterances would be from pupils listening to the discussions and joining in socially but not contributing to the cognitive discourse. They would be acknowledging presence and/or agreement, but they would not be initiating, sustaining or developing the flow of the discussion. Richards observes that "the extent to which they were actually reading the comments is difficult to assess" (104). Both in the physical classroom and the virtual chat room, assessing the learning of the nonparticipatory pupil is difficult and is a major challenge posed by the socially-orientated classroom:

> Chat is becoming an increasingly popular method of communicating for young people. It allows students to gain access to others with similar issues to themselves that are drawn from outside close family or friends. Technology is changing the way that young people behave and interact with others. There has been a trend towards the use of social networking sites that allow students to communicate their feelings, plans and ideas in text form.
>
> (Richards, 2009: 169)

The socially constructed classroom

We now seek empirical evidence supporting the notions of a socially constructed classroom leading to more effective teaching and learning arising from the positive action of teachers to promote a mastery motivational climate. In such classrooms, goal setting in terms of achievement is important. Learners are aware of the priorities and values set by the teacher and the social pressures of the classroom setting. In the study of 1,171 secondary age pupils (Stornes et al., 2008) the researchers explain the classroom interactions and motivations using a framework based upon self-determination theory (Deci and Ryan, 1985; Ryan and Deci, 2000). The underpinning claim is that human beings can either be passive or alienated by the social context or they can be proactive and engaged. The intrinsic motivation, self-regulation and well-being sustained by a positive social context to learning can be enhanced through the social structures of the classroom, which can be fostered by the teacher. The findings of Deci and

Ryan have led to the idea of three innate psychological needs: competence, autonomy and relatedness. When these are satisfied within the classroom, enhanced self-motivation and emotional well-being are likely to follow. If they are not satisfied, learners become demotivated and disengaged.

Stornes' research used questionnaires to gather the empirical evidence about the pupils' perceptions of the teachers' involvement in supporting them as individuals. The pupils were asked to complete the questionnaire in ordinary lesson time under the supervision of their teacher, who read out the questions in turn (to support pupils with learning and/or reading difficulties). The situation was structured to ensure that pupils responded about a single teacher and that others who had completed the questionnaire earlier did not influence the pupils. Factor analysis identified three areas: teacher involvement (care, liking, trust), teacher regulation (rules, expectations, enforcement) and teacher support for autonomy (choice, decision, consideration). The study concludes:

> the social classroom structure may influence the motivational climates . . . a teacher who involves him/herself emphatically with each student may facilitate a mastery motivational climate . . . a mastery motivational climate seems to require a certain amount of influence.
>
> (Stornes *et al.*, 2008: 327)

This has implications for our role as teacher, how we plan our interventions and how we present the curriculum to provide for choice and decision making.

Summary

- Firsthand observation of learning and the surveying of research are both important ways of establishing theory, pedagogy and strategies towards good teaching.
- Learners need to have the skills to learn in a social environment.
- The social and emotional aspects of learning are important.
- Cooperation and collaboration can be established through planning.
- Computer-based activities can foster social constructivist teaching.

Activities

- Consider, in the light of the content of this chapter, the different areas in which social interaction, well-being and learning have been researched.

- Compare the different approaches to research.

- Consider how the research might support particular teaching strategies.

3

Theory

The precepts of social constructivism and social learning theory

By the end of this chapter you will be able to:

- identify the major components of social constructivist and social learning theories as they relate to classrooms;
- identify and contextualise the work of Vygotsky, Bruner, Bandura and Lave and Wenger.

This book is based upon theories which hold, as a central premise, that learning is a social activity.

"Social constructivism has as a central precept that knowledge is created by learners in the context of, and as a result of social interaction" (van Harmelen, 2008: 36). This succinct quote from van Harmelen is actually one of a great many that could have been used to support the point being made. The social constructivist and social learning schools are clear on this point. Learning is a highly social activity.

In this book we are looking at social learning as a totality and although there are subgroups within the wider socially-based theories, we will actually deal with the area as a coherent notion which fully supports the sentiments in van Harmelen's short message.

Social interaction, thinking and engagement

As we have seen, the theory of social constructivism as it relates to learning is predicated almost entirely upon the work of the Russian psychologist Lev Vygotsky. We have also looked at the work of other theorists in this domain. In the following pages we will consider the major elements of the work of those who developed the full range of the social aspects of learning. We will consider these aspects as they can be applied in teaching and learning contexts, either formal or informal, and in their application to situations involving learning where a description of the probable progress of learning, and a consideration of learning behaviours, is called for.

It appears to be widely quoted that Vygotsky said or wrote that "Full cognitive development requires social interaction." This is almost certainly a paraphrase and, although it does represent an important element of Vygotsky's work, the words were not precisely his. What is being conveyed by the sentiment expressed in the sentence is that as human learners, we depend upon social interaction with those around us for the stimulus, challenge and shared activity which work to promote thinking, engagement with ideas and activities and serve to allow for intellectual growth, including the growth of knowledge and understanding.

From Vygotsky's work we see that there are three major pointers towards our understanding of the processes involved in learning in the terms of the social constructivist domain. They are that: the people around the learner have a central role in learning; the people around the learner influence, sometimes deeply, how the learner sees the world; and certain tools affect the way in which learning and intellectual development progresses. These tools can vary in type and quality and include culture, language and other people. There are three categories of tasks which we are able to attempt or undertake, namely those which can be performed independently, those which cannot be performed even with the support of another and those which come between these two extremes and can be performed with some measure of help from others. It is the others who supply the social dimension for learners.

For Vygotsky, cognitive development and language are shaped by a person's interaction with others; children's knowledge, values and attitudes develop through interaction with others; and social interactions increase a child's level of thinking. Vygotsky suggests that teaching and learning are "social activities that take place between social actors in socially constructed situations" (Moore, 2000: 15).

Principles and planes

Vygotsky gives us the following principles:

1. *Cognitive development is limited to a certain range at any given age.* This refers to Vygotsky's well-known notion of the zone of proximal development (ZPD). At any given point in a child's development there is a limit to what can be achieved next. We have seen earlier how this concept can be described and how it relates to both development and to the sort of support that can be offered socially by another who may be more knowledgeable.

2. *Full cognitive development requires social interaction.* Vygotsky's social development theory, we are told, states that "Social interaction plays a fundamental role in the development of cognition" (Kearsley, 1996). Kearsley (1996) continues by saying that "full cognitive development requires social interaction". Lave's situated learning theory, which is based on Vygotsky's social development theory, "emphasizes active perception over concepts and representation" and that "learning requires social interaction and collaboration" (Kearsley, 1996).

To look a little more deeply into the basis of Vygotsky's work we will next examine two further notions: the intrapsychological and the interpsychological. Vygotsky states that

> [e]very function in the child's cultural development appears twice: first, on the social level, and later, on the individual level; first, between people (interpsychological) and then inside the child (intrapsychological). This applies equally to voluntary attention, to logical memory, and to the formation of concepts. All the higher functions originate as actual relationships between individuals.
>
> (Vygotsky, 1978: 57)

These two levels, also described as "planes", are further explained as:

The social plane: This is where development first takes place. The child/learner observes, listens and begins to imitate. The parent/more knowledgeable other steers, makes corrections and provides challenges.

The internal plane: As the child/learner becomes more competent, information becomes internalised.

The development of language is a good example of this. A young child is provided with many opportunities to listen and otherwise observe language in action. Sometimes this is directed at the child; sometimes the child happens to be in the presence of others who are using language. As we have all seen, the young child, with some measure of encouragement, will begin to imitate the patterns of sound that are all around. The other person involved is likely to offer support (by repeating of sounds or words, for example) or present slightly more complex sounds or words to be copied. As the child becomes more familiar with words or phrases, perhaps, the same words and phrases are considered and rehearsed both aloud and, crucially, internally. Language and thought come together and both in the use of language and, more importantly in some respects, cognitive development moves on: "full cognitive development requires social interaction" (Tu, 2000: 33).

Below are important considerations from the work of Vygotsky to be borne in mind when planning for learning and when teaching:

- Learning and development is a social and collaborative activity which cannot really be taught. For some people this comes easily, especially if they are social in their day-to-day lives and find mixing and talking with others straightforward. Individual learners in the classroom construct their own understanding. During the process of constructing meaning and understanding, the teacher's role is to act as facilitator.

- Being aware of the ZPD and being fully aware that for each learner the zone will be different is crucial for the teacher when planning appropriate tasks and activities which will optimise learning. This knowledge will also inform the teacher of the nature and extent of the support for the learner which should be provided.

- Learning tasks and activities and other learning situations must be set in meaningful contexts. A meaningful context for an adult teacher is not necessarily as meaningful for a young learner. It is highly desirable that the context in which the learning is developed is the same as the context in which the knowledge is to be used.

- If at all possible, in-school learning should be related to out-of-school learning and other experiences. Anything brought to the learning setting by a child (e.g. a picture, an artefact of any kind, or a personal story) can be capitalised upon and integrated into planned learning experiences. This will serve to create a sense of continuity and help to dissipate what can sometimes appear as a gulf between school and real life.

- Most essentially, Vygotsky argues that language is the key to all development. Knowledge and use of words play a central part not only in the development of children's thought but in all aspects of cognitive development.

Looking more broadly at learning as essentially a social activity, taking into account the important notions from across the range of theory, we can produce a set of important principles to complement those taken directly from Vygotsky.

Social interaction is of paramount importance. Such interactivity can be vertical, as in teacher–student interaction, or horizontal, as in student–student interaction. Each kind of interaction has its own effects on learning, with the former emphasizing deep integration of detail and the latter emphasizing elaboration and metacognitive awareness.

Scaffolding: planned and opportunistic

The range and type of support given to learners is a crucial element in the progress of their learning. As we have considered, scaffolding is a means by which a "helper" (broadly defined to be anyone in a position to provide this support) has the potential to provide something which is likely to assist in the process of acquiring knowledge and developing understanding. Scaffolding is measured and appropriate intervention which has the purpose of enabling a learner to move forward.

It is possible, though not entirely necessary, to consider two different approaches to scaffolding. First, scaffolding can be planned intervention. This implies that a teacher – planned intervention is most likely to have been planned by a teacher – will have made a decision to provide a means to assist progress towards preplanned learning outcomes. This may consist of a range of different approaches, more detail of which will be considered later. Some examples might be the provision of a word bank for a child using a word processor, simplified instructions/explanations for individuals or personal attention from the teacher or another adult – this could be continuing or intermittent. Naturally, there are many other approaches to providing scaffolded support. Some involve human intervention; others involve the provision of materials or the opportunity to interact with peers or even a computer program.

Second, we have what can be called "ad hoc" interventions. These opportunities for scaffolding are more difficult to plan. They depend upon the teacher/adult being in the right place at the right time in many cases, the informed professional judgement of the adult in other situations or a group situation when dialogue is being developed between an adult and the class. Often, the nature of any intervention can be crucial. It can vary from a short and concise question to something more elaborate, such as suggesting a further source of information or a different approach to solving a problem. The emphasis must be on support and development rather than on giving answers. An adage which reflects this and is sometimes used to make the point is "Telling is not teaching". This adage is sometimes linked to the adage "Hearing is not learning". Both of these imply that opportunities for dialogue, thought, action and an engagement with ideas underlie the process of learning.

Attention to the process of intervention is given importance in the materials provided by the National Strategies, a long-standing initiative to raise standards in teaching and learning in the UK (see Figure 3.1). By using

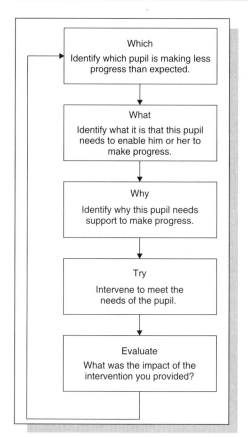

Figure 3.1 Planning for intervention
Source: Adapted from National Strategies, 2009

a set of questions as starting points, teachers are encouraged to gauge their intervention to make the best impact on the progress of the learner.

As we will see, there is a wide range of variety in the scope and nature of scaffolding as it is employed in practice. The purpose of scaffolding is to support the learner in an attempt to achieve higher levels of development by a means of different approaches. The teacher, as scaffolder, can take on different roles in order to provide scaffolding, for example:

- *teacher as support*: providing a secure framework and safe context where children feel able to make suggestions and try out ideas;
- *teacher as prompt*: using questions to redirect the individual learner's thinking or providing alternative, possibly simpler, language;
- *teacher as critical listener and provider of feedback*: giving critical comment in a form which is understandable by the learner and might suggest pursuing the tack being taken or perhaps looking elsewhere;
- *teacher as simplifier*: breaking a problem into smaller more manageable steps to be tackled by the learner;

- *teacher as motivator*: giving appropriate encouragement at critical points in a process;
- *teacher as highlighter*: pointing out aspects of a task or question which demand more attention than other less significant aspects;
- *teacher as model*: carrying out a task or thinking aloud to demonstrate an approach or technique.

Scaffolding can be characterised as intervention. The waves model, which refers to personalising pedagogical approaches to teaching, sets out the features of effective interventions:

- The teaching is focused and structured so that children and young people know what is to be learned and how it fits with what they know and can do already.
- Learners are motivated with pace, dialogue and stimulating activities.
- Learners' progress is assessed regularly, using practitioner-led assessment, self-assessment and peer-assessment approaches that enable subsequent sessions to be tailored to their needs.
- Lessons or sessions are designed around a structure that emphasises the stages of learning from which children and young people will most benefit.
- Teachers create a settled and purposeful atmosphere for learning.
- Teachers have high expectations of the effort learners will need to make.
- Teaching concentrates on the misconceptions, gaps or weaknesses that learners have had with earlier work and builds in some extra consolidation.

(National Strategies, 2007: 12)

In a small-scale study which investigated approaches to encouraging primary-aged children to develop the use of focused questions in their science work, it was found that by using a consistent approach making full use of scaffolding, modelling and prompting techniques in an environment of safety (i.e. an environment in which the trying out of new ideas and expressing personal opinions was encouraged and never disregarded or discounted out of hand), teachers helped children to develop sophisticated questioning techniques.

Children who learned through the use of scaffolding strategies by their teachers seemed to show sustained interest, were more focused and also retained a deeper level of understanding (Agar *et al.*, 2006).

The importance and heritage of scaffolding is summed up in a recent UK government publication which is a part of the National Strategy aimed at raising standards of both teaching and pupil attainment:

The concept of scaffolding in teaching serves a similar purpose to the scaffolding constructed around a building to make it safe and accessible.

When the job has been done, the scaffolding is removed and the new or reconstructed building stands in its own right. Teachers can use scaffolding techniques to teach a specific aspect of basic skills. They construct a "scaffold" around the area so that learners have direct access to the chosen focus, with nothing allowed to get in the way. To be of benefit, scaffolding must be temporary. When the learner shows signs of handling the task in question, the "scaffolding" can then be removed gradually until it is no longer needed. In this way, "handover" is achieved; without this part in the process, scaffolding would breed dependence and helplessness. Scaffolding enables learners to reach beyond their current competencies and explore new understandings and skills.

(DCSF, 2009b)

Modelling and thinking aloud

By modelling certain activities, teachers or others can provide opportunities for learners to observe and then imitate and replicate. This does not simply apply to practical or other physical skills, although in sports coaching situations, for example, this can be seen quite obviously. It also applies in many other situations, for example reading, writing and working out calculations. By providing a commentary during the activity to be modelled, attention can be drawn to the essential elements of the task in question. We can see that this relates closely to the common elements of the works of Bandura, Lave and Wenger that have been considered earlier.

To sum up this section relating to the nature and importance of scaffolding as a pedagogical tool motivated by social constructivism and social learning theory, Figure 3.2 sets out five activities which a scaffolder might choose to implement in the course of supporting individuals or groups of learners.

Extending the principles of social constructivism

Three principles of constructivism, upon which both social constructivism and other social learning theory can be seen to be founded, are presented by Bruner (1966). They are:

- Teaching must be concerned with the experiences and contexts that make the learner willing and able to learn (i.e. readiness).
- Teaching must be structured so that it can be easily grasped by the learner.

Figure 3.2 Scaffolding techniques
Source: Adapted from TADHD, 2009

■ Teaching should be designed to facilitate extrapolation and/or fill in the gaps (i.e. go beyond the information given).

Following on from this, and in an attempt to draw together a set of principles which apply across the spectrum of socially mediated learning, the following principles can be distilled from the broad arena of social constructivism and social learning theory in general (Deaux *et al.*, 1993; Ormond, 1999):

■ It is possible to learn by observing the behaviour of others and the outcomes of their behaviour. Bandura (1997a) puts this point into context:

> Learning would be exceedingly laborious, not to mention hazardous, if people had to rely solely on the effects of their own actions to inform them what to do. Fortunately, most human behaviour is learned observationally through modelling: from observing others one forms an idea

of how new behaviours are performed, and on later occasions this coded information serves as a guide for action.

(Bandura, 1997a: 22)

- Cognition plays a central role in learning; learning is not simply a question of stimulus and response. Social learning theory places cognitive engagement at the hub of human learning. However, the theory also acknowledges that an expectation of future reinforcement or punishment can have an effect on behaviour.
- In some ways, social learning theory is looked upon as a bridge connecting behaviourist and cognitive learning theories.

To end this chapter we should consider the words of Jean Lave, the originator of the apprenticeship explanation of social learning:

Cognitive apprenticeship supports learning in a domain by enabling students to acquire, develop and use cognitive tools in authentic domain activity. Learning, both outside and inside school, advances through collaborative social interaction and the social construction of knowledge.

(Lave, 1998: 134)

Summary

- Learning is a highly social activity. (There are, of course, notable exceptions to this statement at the level of some individual learners' preferences.)
- Knowledge is created by learners in the context of and as a result of social interaction (van Harmelen, 2008).

Activities

- Consider, in the light of the content of this chapter, the different aspects of social learning and the way in which the theories may indicate the efficacy of particular teaching strategies.
- Consider the scaffolding strategies that you have used, or witnessed being used, in teaching.

4

Pedagogy

The rules, principles and theories that guide current practice

By the end of this chapter you will be able to:

- identify the theories of pedagogy relating to the social classroom;
- identify approaches that are designed to support learning in a social classroom;
- identify the basis for planning teaching with regard to social constructivist theories.

In this chapter, we consider pedagogy in the area of the social classroom, that is, how teachers can operate within the theory. We have seen that constructivist teaching is based on the belief that learning occurs when the learner constructs his or her own knowledge and understanding. Learning is an active process that means that the learner must actively participate in the process; learning does not occur when the learner passively receives information. Learners are the makers of meaning and knowledge, not simply the receivers.

The characteristics of a constructivist pedagogy

Constructivist teaching is associated with learning that is made up from some or all of the following: critical thinking, motivation, learner independence, feedback, dialogue, language, explanation, questioning, learning through teaching, contextualisation, experiments and/or real-world problem solving. These aspects of learning will be considered later and also reflected in Chapter 5 in a selection of vignette case studies.

The constructivist teacher is one who values learner reflection and cognitive conflict and encourages peer interaction (ACT, 2007). Bruner (1966) states that the method of instruction should address four major aspects: predisposition towards learning, the ways in which a body of knowledge can be structured so that it can be most readily grasped by the learner, the most effective sequences in which to present material, and the nature and pacing of rewards and punishments. Good methods for structuring knowledge should result in simplifying concepts, generating new propositions and increasing the manipulation of information. It is these skills of teachers that enable learning to take place.

Pedagogy is the heart of teaching. It is the rules and principles that guide effective and efficient activities which lead to learning. It is described equally as an art form and as a science. "Paidagōgos" is an ancient Greek word (παιδαγωγός) meaning "a slave who takes children to school to learn". That idea is almost at odds with the current idea of pedagogy enabling learners to learn, but it does remind us that it is "working with children and providing the opportunity to learn" and so the less rigorous meaning "child-leading" is more appropriate to our current understanding of the process. Pedagogy is about teaching methods and principles of instruction. It is assisting students through interaction and activity in the ongoing academic and social events of the classroom.

In contrast, andragogy consists of teaching strategies and principles of instruction focusing on adults and is seen as engaging adult learners with the structure of the learning experience. The German educator Alexander Kapp first used the term "andragogy" (man-leading) in 1833 to describe the differences between working with adults and working with children. The ideas were developed into a theory of adult education by Malcolm Knowles. He asserted that andragogy should be distinguished from pedagogy because the nature of learning and the motivations to learn were different and that any experience which adults perceive as putting them in the position of being treated as children is bound to interface with their learning (Knowles, 1970).

Knowles refers to pedagogy as "the art and science of teaching children" (Knowles, 1980: 43), but he refers to andragogy as "the art and science of helping adults to learn" (43). Many of the principles of andragogy grew from those of pedagogy, but they acknowledged the differences in adults from children and included real-world contextualisation, learner ownership, self-determination, learning enriched by prior experience and a readiness and orientation to learning. That was over 30 years ago. In many ways, those principles of andragogy have been readopted by pedagogy in the enlightened, post-modern movement of classroom-based learning. Knowles' work (based on Knowles, 1990: 57) can be interpreted and developed as:

- learners need to know why they are learning;

- learners need to be in control of how and when to learn;

- learners can use their worldly experiences to support the learning process;

- learners are more ready to learn when learning is contextualised;

- learners are motivated to learn real-life tasks, skills and understanding;

- learners are motivated by acknowledged success.

It is interesting to note here that Knowles is not alone in defining pedagogy as both an art and a science. Many educationalists have used this conjunction of two notions – one giving an impression of high technology and the other suggesting a more aesthetic or creative enterprise. See, as examples, Brine (2009), Venkataiah (1998) and Dunkin (1987); there are many others.

A further aspect of teaching relating to pedagogy has arisen through the application of educational technology. It is called "cybergogy" (computers leading the learning) and relates to the principles and practice of teaching through the internet. The Wang model of cybergogy places engaged learning at the intersection of social, emotive and cognitive factors, where the cognitive factors are prior knowledge, goals, activity and learning style; the social factors are personality, context, community and communication; and the emotive factors relate to feelings about self, community, learning and the environment (Wang, 2007; Wang and Kang, 2006).

Definitions of cybergogy attempt to combine the principles of pedagogy and andragogy. They acknowledge that cybergogy is applicable to both adults and children: "Many youths and young adults are embracing cyberspace and cyber learning without giving it a second thought. To them cyber learning will be just another education delivery system that connects them to the world" (Carrier and Moulds, 2003: 4). The new approach to learning focuses on helping adults, young people and children to learn by providing the opportunities through technology and structured experience. The principles include those of andragogy: enabling learner-centred, autonomous and contextualised learning. But, despite the similarities and borrowed principles, there needs to be an acknowledgement that strategies used for face-to-face and book-orientated learning at whatever age may not be the same as those guiding teaching in the virtual environment.

The concept of cybergogy has been developed further to guide the structure and presentation of online activities. The model embraces four learning domains – cognitive, emotional, dextrous and social – and represents activities as learning archetypes (Scopes, 2009: 22) which facilitate learning experiences which are enhanced by and, in some cases, made possible only by the very nature of the multiuser, virtual environments.

We have seen that constructivist teaching is based on the belief that learning occurs when the learner constructs their personal knowledge and understanding and that it has to be an active process on behalf of the learner. The social constructivist believes that the learning takes place through language and the dialogue between two or more learners. All constructivists support a pedagogy that promotes teaching techniques which build upon knowledge and concepts which learners already know or understand; this prior knowledge is called a "schema" or "mental structure" that represents some aspect of the world. We have seen in Chapter 1 that the term "schema" was first used by Piaget. Subsequent psychologists have used the idea to represent the structures of prior and current knowledge and understanding (Anderson, 1983; Armbruster, 1996; Bartlett, 1932; Bransford, 1979; Brewer and Treyens, 1981; Freundschuh and Sharma, 1996; Halliday and Hassan, 1989). This theory of learning views organised knowledge as an elaborate network of abstract mental structures which represent understanding of the world. A strong element of schema representation arises from the study of metaphor: "My chief point has been to show that these image schemata are pervasive, well-defined, and of sufficient internal structure to constrain our understanding and reasoning" (Johnson, 1987: 128). The connections between visual imagery and schema memory are strong (Clausner and Croft, 1997; Lakoff and Johnson, 1980; Richardson *et al.*, 2001; Rohrer, 1995; Woollard, 2004a).

Further, constructivist teaching seeks to provide an environmentally rich, problem-solving context that encourages the learner's investigation, invention, insight and inference. Learning does not occur when the learner passively receives information. This is interpreted in the most general sense as encouraging learners to use active techniques, such as experiments and real-world problem solving, to create more knowledge and then to reflect on and to talk about what they are doing, thinking and understanding.

In the constructivist classroom, the learners are the makers of meaning and knowledge. Learners are not empty vessels into which knowledge and wisdom (dating back to Plutarch in the first century AD) is poured. Learners are not blank slates (i.e. Locke's tabula rasa) on which the runes of time are written. Importantly, knowledge and understanding are not communicated without the learner making sense of it according to his or her current conceptions. Therefore, learning best takes place when learners are allowed to construct a personal understanding based on experiencing things and reflecting on those experiences. Good methods for structuring knowledge should result in simplifying concepts, generating new propositions and increasing the manipulation of information. Constructivist teaching is associated with learning that involves critical thinking, motivation, learner independence, feedback, dialogue, language, explanation, Socratic-style questioning, learning through teaching, contextualisation, experiments and real-world problem solving.

The pedagogy arising from the consideration of andragogy, cybergogy and the constructivist learning theory can be summarised as a number of principles for teacher actions. These actions can take place before, during and after the learning takes place. Teachers should:

- tell the learners why they are learning;
- provide opportunities to make the learner feel in control;
- provide opportunities for active engagement (cognitive, kinaesthetic and social);
- plan to use the learners' previous experiences;
- plan to structure the learning experience based upon understanding of the curriculum;
- engage with the learners through dialogue and questioning;
- be sensitive to the emotional aspects of learning experiences;
- contextualise the activities with real-life examples.

The diversity of activity for the teacher in the social classroom is the major feature. The provision of opportunity and the responsiveness to individual need is the major challenge. Doing, talking, challenging, experimenting and exploring are the major activities.

The social constructivist teacher values learner reflection, cognitive conflict and peer interaction. The constructivist teacher understands the learners' pre-existing conceptions and guides the activities to support them and then build upon them.

Being prepared for learning

With appropriate support, learners can often perform tasks that they are incapable of completing on their own. Scaffolding, as we have seen – where the teacher continually adjusts the level of his or her support in response to the learner's level of performance – is an effective form of teaching. Scaffolding not only produces immediate results but also instils the skills necessary for independent problem solving in the future. But, before the learner can enter this world of self-perpetuating experience, they must be prepared for learning.

Jerome Bruner states that a theory of instruction should address four major aspects: (1) being prepared for learning; (2) the ways in which a body of knowledge can be structured so that it can be most readily grasped by the learner; (3) the most effective sequences in which to present material; and (4) the nature and pacing of rewards and punishments. This section considers the learner's predisposition towards learning. Learning does not take place in isolation; it is not a spontaneous act. Learning needs stimulus, context and structure. Also, learning needs the learner to be prepared for learning (Bruner, 1966).

Lev Vygotsky focused on children's cognitive development when considering their preparedness for learning. Notably, he suggested that a learner might evidence one level of skill independently, but with appropriate support the same learner could show a higher level of functioning. Vygotsky (see Chapter 1) called this the "zone of proximal development" (ZPD) (Vygotsky, 1978). He identified that the support was social in nature and that parents, teachers or even peers might act as the support to extend the learning.

Jean Piaget (1970) proffered ideas of assimilation and accommodation. He argued that as the learner meets new experiences that go beyond existing levels of understanding, the existing concepts are stretched to accommodate the new data or ideas.

In Jerome Bruner's proposals there is a spiral curriculum and the learner learns at the point of their understanding. He argues that instructions need to be appropriate to the learner's logical abilities (i.e. within their grasp). Importantly for this consideration of pedagogy, he proposes that intellectual development of the learner is not a clockwork sequence of events. The teacher "need not follow slavishly the natural course of cognitive development in the child. It can also lead to intellectual development by providing challenging but usable opportunities for the child to forge ahead in his development" (Bruner, 1960: 147).

Malcolm Knowles' ideas of preparedness arise not from a cognitive perspective, but from a social or personal perspective. In andragogy, being prepared for learning relates to an appreciation of the importance of the content and acceptance of the context.

The pedagogy arising from the consideration of preparedness for learning can be summarised as a number of principles of teacher actions. Those actions can be carried out before, during and after the learning takes place. Teachers should:

- be aware of what the learner can do unaided;
- be aware of what the learner understands;
- be prepared for the teaching activity;
- establish the importance of the content of learning;
- have aspirations of what could be achieved (i.e. be able to estimate the ZPD);
- provide challenges within the ZPD;
- provide sequential structures of the content;
- reflect upon the learners' responses to the activities.

The social constructivist teacher is prepared to accommodate individuals' learning. The constructivist teacher knows the content of the curriculum and the structures and sequences and understands the learners' pre-existing conceptions and guides the activities to support them and then build upon them.

Structure, sequence and alternatives

The pedagogy supporting constructivist approaches is concerned with structuring knowledge (i.e. the curriculum) and the experiences introducing that knowledge to ensure the generation of new propositions and an increase in the manipulation of information. There is a distinct contrast between this approach and the didactic, analytical and objective characteristics of behaviourist approaches which also support a highly structured methodology. The structuring for constructivist approaches requires attention to the differently held beliefs and understandings of the learner; the structuring process needs to accommodate those differences.

There are also differences between the idea that learners go through stages of development and acquire cognitive skills by the passage of time and experience and the idea that each learner is on an individual path which has no predetermined requirements or prerequisites. Jerome Bruner's claim that "any subject can be taught effectively in some intellectually honest form to any child at any stage of development" (1960: 33) underpins the need for the constructivist pedagogy to be flexible in dealing with both the individual learner and the curriculum. An important aspect of the structuring is the long-term revisiting of the curriculum; the same subject should be introduced early but reintroduced repeatedly at later stages. This is consistent with the point that there is an imperfect relationship between intellectual progress and chronological age.

This example is taken from Bruner:

> The concept of prime numbers appears to be more readily grasped when the child, through construction, discovers that certain handfuls of beans cannot be laid out in completed rows and columns. Such quantities have either to be laid out in a single file or in an incomplete row-column design in which there is always one extra or one too few to fill the pattern. These patterns, the child learns, happen to be called prime. It is easy for the child to go from this step to the recognition that a multiple table, so called, is a record sheet of quantities in completed multiple rows and columns. Here is factoring, multiplication and primes in a construction that can be visualized.
>
> (TIPS, 2009)

In this example, Bruner identifies the value of visualisation in understanding. It also relates to the use of metaphor in understanding (Lakoff and Johnson, 1980; Rohrer, 1995; Woollard, 2004a) and other mental models approaches to understanding (Anderson, 1983; Eysenck and Eysenck, 1969; Gentner and Stevens, 1983; Holland *et al.*, 1986; Kelly, 1995).

Sequencing experience is an important aspect of the structuring process, but no one sequencing will fit every learner. The constructivist teacher develops sequences for teaching based on general principles which are then applied flexibly in response to the individual learners. Sequencing, or lack of it, can make learning easier or more difficult.

This discussion of structure and sequence may give the misleading impression that constructivist approaches are definite, inflexible, predetermined and absolute. That is far from the truth. The structure and sequence considerations are necessary to ensure that the activities closely, but not exactly, match where the learner is successfully operating. This next discussion focuses upon how the learning is accommodated and stimulated though enriching the sequence and structure through the presentation of alternatives.

The environment in which learning takes place is important and there is a natural assumption that in the constructivist classroom there is ample opportunity for communication or dialogue. Structuring dialogue is not an easy task and the analysis of the situation below is designed to help identify those strategies that will promote effective dialogue. There are four forms of dialogue proposed: that which asserts or defines the learning structure; that which raises alternatives, contractions and challenges; that which seeks to continue or extend the dialogue; and that which confirms or affirms the learning.

Assertions include:

- definition of terms;
- introductions, statements of expectations, fears and learners' current thinking;
- setting the agenda, defining the scope, describing the context;
- starter activities, warm-up activities and engagements (preparedness to learn);
- teacher planning may include learning outcomes and objectives and phases/transitions within the learning session.

Contradictions include:

- brainstorm, ideas shower and spider diagrams;
- tutor/teacher contributions;
- debate.

Continuations include:

- teacher-planned phases and transitions;
- advanced organisers;
- action planning;
- roles within groups (e.g. chair, secretary, etc.).

Confirmations include:

- group presentations;
- assignment writing;
- hot seating;

- tests and teacher assessment questioning;
- summary, plenary and closure.

Arguably, the most important form of dialogue is argument. When the learner enters into a dialogue about their understanding, they are reinforcing their beliefs and being swayed by the beliefs of another. The support from theory for argument, debate and questioning is strong. Any pedagogic approach should embrace the opportunities for open and honest discourse about the content of the curriculum. Brooks and Brooks (1993) recommend providing opportunities for disequilibrium (see Chapter 1 on Piaget's genetic epistemology) to occur. They state that these opportunities are more effective for clarifying understanding than alternatives, such as trying to explain verbally the flaw in an individual's understanding: "Teachers who operate without awareness of their students' points of view often doom students to dull, irrelevant experiences, and even failure" (60).

There is a similar debate regarding argument and learner interaction and the benefits of healthy disagreement in the online learning world. There are new pedagogical scenarios arising from the use of synchronous communication, such as instant messaging and chat rooms. The online learning experience need not simply involve a lone learner at a keyboard exploring predetermined material and responding to computer-presented questions that are marked right or wrong. Computer-supported collaborative learning (CSCL) supports the social constructivist pedagogy whereby learners interact and grow their understanding by questioning, proposing, arguing and agreeing. Andriessen *et al.* (2003) in *Arguing to Learn: Confronting Cognitions in Computer-Supported Collaborative Learning Environments* draw together many of the traditional theories of learning and principles of pedagogy and relate them to the online or virtual learning environments.

Controlling the discussion and argument between learners in a traditional classroom environment can be a significant challenge. The role of the teacher is to manage that discussion and a powerful strategy is Socratic questioning. Socrates (*c.*470–399 BC), the early Greek philosopher and teacher, provides the name for a pedagogic approach that promotes questioning based on the practice of disciplined (within the bounds of the normal social discourse), rigorous (depth of knowledge/understanding), systematic (structured within the scope and context) and thoughtful (reflecting upon previous responses) dialogue. Socratic questioning is about challenging beliefs by seeking rationalisation and justification.

The pedagogic approach of Socratic questioning has three purposes. First, this form of questioning is an assessment opportunity. It is possible to probe learner thinking, to help identify what they know or understand from what they do not know or understand and to identify errors and misconceptions. Second, the process helps the learner to begin to distinguish what they know or understand from what they do not know or understand. Third, the process helps to promote learners' abilities to ask Socratic questions and to help students acquire the powerful tools of Socratic dialogue to support future learning. Preparing to lead a Socratic discussion requires the teacher to apply the questioning techniques (i.e. questioning should be disciplined, systematic, rigorous and thoughtful) internally. From the initial topic, the thought processes need to be systematic and rigorous. The systematic aspect clearly defines the scope of the questions and identifies important elements of the context and, in the main, is determined by the curriculum. The rigour arises from the depth of questioning (i.e. the detail and the complexity of that detail) and is largely determined by the intellectual capability of the learners.

During the Socratic discussion, the teacher should draw upon different sorts of questions to develop and steer the dialogue. Some questions are designed to clarify the concept under discussion, perhaps requiring the learner to rephrase their thoughts, but importantly getting them to say more, to colour their thoughts and enrich the idea (clarification). Others seek the evidence for those ideas (justification), sometimes by probing the assumptions (validation). Some questions challenge the learner to consider contradictory, complementary or different points of view (consideration) to bring a better understanding.

Clarification: What exactly does that mean? Can you rephrase that? How does that fit in? What is that like? Who does that involve? Where is that? How does that relate to . . .? What is the evidence? When does that happen? When is it true? What does that mean?

Justification: What is the evidence for . . .? Who says that . . .? How do you know . . .? Can you give an example of . . .? Why does that happen . . .? Why did I ask that question?

Validation: Are you assuming . . .? Why are you assuming . . .? Is that assumption correct? What assumptions are you making?

Consideration: What about . . . [an alternative]? How does that compare with . . .? What about other people's ideas? Why not . . .? Is that better than . . .? Isn't [an alternative] better?

Along with these strategies there are overarching principles of planning learning sessions in a constructivist classroom. The introductory elements should be sound, stable, known, accepted and correct. Before the end of the learning session, the dialogue will have become more unpredictable, wide-ranging, less familiar, more controversial or contentious and more prone to error or misconception. These changes throughout the lesson are at various levels and are expressed on the scales of concepts, focus, content, risk taking and complexity:

- *Concepts*: concrete to abstract, for example, identifying the accessibility features of a web page to judging the accessibility of a website.

- *Focus*: precise to general, for example, analysing and identifying features of a good web page leading to the learners identifying their rules for designing web pages.

- *Content*: familiar to novel, for example, identifying previously discussed features of good web pages and leading to a broader or deeper identification of web page design principles.

- *Risk taking*: low to high, for example, the teacher making value judgements and presenting them to the class and leading to learners presenting their ideas and being challenged by peers (hot seating).

- *Complexity*: simple to complex, for example, reading and applying rules of design to articulating rules derived from classroom experience.

In each of these examples there appears to be a linear sequence of activity and this discussion of sequencing, by the nature of its presentation, appears to be a linear process. Yet, as we have seen, many theories of learning are cyclic or spiral in nature (Bruner, 1960; Jarvis *et al.*, 2003; Kolb, 1984). And so, the pedagogy must also reflect that cyclic nature. Cycles occur on the macro scale and cycles occur on the micro scale; they occur at the level of schemes of work and at the level of single dialogues between learners. The concept of sequencing activities must also reflect the cyclical nature of learning and the repetitive nature of teaching.

The pedagogy arising from the consideration of structure, sequence and alternatives can be summarised as a number of principles of teacher actions. Teachers should:

- ensure that the learner is willing and able to learn;

- provide structure to the learning process by sequencing activities from the simple to the more complex (spiral structure);

- provide representation, description and explanation of concepts as the basis for learning;
- recognise the power of visual representation;
- provide opportunities to explore the concepts and, in particular, present the contradictions, alternatives, interpolations and extrapolations;
- give control to the learner to create their structure and sequence;
- confirm the new concepts through presentation, assessment and celebration;
- consider the opportunities offered by online synchronous dialogue.

The social constructivist teacher must know the learners, but it is also important that they know the curriculum and its structure and sequence and how that curriculum can be presented in different ways to accommodate the complexities and diversities of understanding of the content.

Cognitive apprenticeship

Another aspect of the pedagogy of the social classroom arises from the consideration of cognitive apprenticeship (see Chapter 3). Discussions of cooperation and collaboration in the classroom often make the assumption that any common goal set for learners is to be pursued collaboratively by learners of equal status. Alternatively, other studies into small group work, independently of the collaborative or cooperative nature of the relationships, talk about roles and responsibilities that learners may adopt. The basis of cognitive apprenticeship is that one person is acting as the guide for the other person.

The proponents of the cognitive apprenticeship theory and resulting pedagogy cite previous practice. Cognitive apprenticeships follow a historic model based upon successful craft apprenticeships typical of the craft guilds of the Middle Ages, those supplying skilled workers to drive the industrial revolution, those in post-war Britain offering "a sheltered and extended period in which the young person was able to grow up and become job-ready" (Vickerstaff, 2007: 331) and probably, in the same way, those in which skills and knowledge have been passed from generation to generation for eons. Cognitive apprenticeship is the process whereby a master of a skill teaches that skill to an apprentice. Cognitive apprenticeships "try to enculturate students into authentic practices" (Brown *et al.*, 1989: 32); this could be interpreted as contextualised learning or situated learning (see Chapter 3). It can also be aligned with legitimate peripheral participation (see Chapter 1), a theoretical description of how newcomers to a group become experienced members and eventually elders of a community of practice (COP) or collaborative project.

Applying an apprenticeship method to cognitive skills rather than physical skills requires the externalisation (i.e. expression through language) of processes which are usually carried out internally through thought alone. The apprentice, by observing the processes expressed by the master, is better able to carry out those thought processes independently and internally (Collins *et al.*, 1989: 457–548). The pedagogy is based upon modelling, that is, the apprentice copying or adapting the actions of the master. This approach is supported by Albert Bandura's theory of modelling as a means of learning. To be successful, the learner must be attentive, must be observant, must recall the observed, must be motivated and must be able (Bandura, 1997a and 1997b).

The position of the master in the arrangement is interesting. If, under the normal circumstances of the classroom, he or she is a peer of the apprentice, they are a "peer master". The following considerations are worthy of discussion:

- As a result of the peer master's knowledge, understanding and interest, the apprentice may have a more positive relationship to the subject matter, perceive it to have a higher value and be better prepared for learning.

- The apprentice may have a stronger, more positive, more socially engaged relationship with the peer master than with the teacher.

- The peer master may be better placed to contextualise the concepts than the teacher. The master may be better placed to articulate the concepts in the idiom of the learner than the teacher.

- The peer master may gain more understanding of the content through the act of repeating the processes and rehearsing the content so the peer master gains better understanding through the process.

- The peer master may gain more understanding of the content through creating new words and resources to describe the content – there are connections with learning through authoring.

As we have seen, there are many advantages in placing a learner in a teacher position, but the positive aspects of cognitive apprenticeship need to be considered in light of a number of issues and challenges. Namely:

- While peer masters are teaching, they are not necessarily learning; their thoughts are being focused on their apprentice's learning and not their own.

- It is very challenging for teachers to match content and presentation of content to individual learners. The challenge is far more complex if it is to match peer master to apprentice.

- The supply of sufficient peer masters of any particular content to the number of apprentices may be insufficient.

- The teacher's identification of peer masters within the classroom is a challenging task.

- How do we know they are masters? Who trains the masters? When do the masters learn other things?

The above discussion has focused on the role in the social classroom of a peer taking on the role of master in the master–apprentice relationship. However, the theory and pedagogy arising also applies to the teacher being the master. This theory does acknowledge that masters of a skill or concept do not necessarily consider the implicit processes involved in carrying out complex skills or the prerequisites of understanding the concept when working with learners. The big question regarding the cognitive apprentice theory and resulting pedagogy relates to the observation that knowledge of a subject does not automatically imply ability to teach that subject. It is "not just knowing it but knowing how to teach it" (Woollard, 2004b: 17). This issue has been thoroughly explored by Lee Shuman and his construct, pedagogic content knowledge (PCK). As teachers, our challenge is to enable learners to gain the skills, knowledge and understanding that we possess. The challenge to teachers is to also teach an ever-changing curriculum in terms of content (i.e. knowledge), concepts and skills. We then have to develop the means by which we teach subject content knowledge. Lee Shulman calls this the "pedagogical content knowledge" (Shulman, 1987). He observes sharp contrasts in the teaching paradigms through history, notably the change from the late nineteenth-century emphasis upon content through phases until the current time of pupil-centred learning, meeting individual needs, cultural awareness, understanding youth, classroom management, behaviour modification, instructional materials and adherence to educational policies and procedures. There is a growing body of thought that now turns the emphasis of good teaching towards the process of changing knowledge into knowing how to teach the knowledge. In the cognitive apprentice model it is important that the master possesses the appropriate subject knowledge, skills, understanding and, equally importantly, the pedagogic knowledge relating to that content.

The underpinning requirement when developing a pedagogy based upon cognitive apprenticeships is that they ". . . are designed, among other things, to bring these tacit processes into the open, where students can observe, enact, and practice them with help from the teacher . . ." (Collins *et al.*, 1989: 458). In contemporary teaching, coaching, or teaching expertise, enables the learner to perfect skills and understanding by having physical movements or verbal articulation of their ideas continually honed through instruction, advice and discourse. The acquisition of skills can be said to go through the three stages of the cognitive, the associative and the autonomous (Anderson, 1983):

- *Cognitive*: novices forming their understanding of the concept or application of the skills by observation, discourse or instruction.
- *Associative*: learners can apply the skill or understand the concept but are still gaining through practice, dialogue and thought.
- *Autonomous*: the learner as an expert completes the activity or uses the concept in a way that appears automatic, embedded and effortless.

(Based on Fitts and Posner, 1967; Vereijken, 1991)

Finally, the value of all pedagogy is to enable the learner to be independent. That independence is in terms of both the acquired knowledge, understanding and skills and independence in terms of the ability of the learner to acquire new knowledge and understanding and skills. An important aspect of the cognitive apprentice method is the articulation, reflection and exploration of the learned material. It is important that the master enables the apprentice to articulate their knowledge, reasoning and problem-solving processes in the same way as the master articulated them for the apprentice. The reflection element is the ability of the learner to compare the newly-acquired skills with alternatives expressed by others. Exploration requires the apprentice to experiment, trial, pilot and research other methods. A good master will guarantee that these processes are enabled to ensure independence and the apprentice reaching the autonomous stage where the learner's skill becomes honed and perfected until it is executed at an expert level (Anderson, 2000) with the potential of the apprentice becoming a master.

An implication arising from the use of cognitive apprentice techniques is the need to establish record keeping of attainment in the key knowledge, concepts and skills areas of the curriculum in question. For any particular classroom activity, skill development or curriculum concept, learners can be placed in one of four categories. More able learners are those who have achieved fluency in the activity, skill or concept. The most able can teach the activity, skills or concept to an apprentice. Some learners work towards fluency and are in their ZPD. The least able are potential apprentices for the masters in the group (see Figure 4.1).

The pedagogy arising from the consideration of cognitive apprenticeship can be summarised as a number of principles of teacher actions. Teachers should:

- identify potential masters in a specific activity, skill or concept;
- identify potential apprentices in a specific activity, skill or concept;
- identify the extra tuition needed by a more able learner to enable them to be a peer master;
- when supporting learners, make provision to enable them to progress from the cognitive through the associate to the autonomous stage;
- emphasise the importance of verbal articulation of the activity, skills or cognitive processes by the peer master;
- emphasise the importance of verbal articulation of the activity, skills or cognitive processes by the apprentice.

The social constructivist teacher must be aware of the values of cognitive apprenticeship and the implications for utilising the knowledge, understanding and skills of the learners in their charge.

Social interaction and classroom talking

A challenge for teachers can be enabling learners to talk, that is, enabling and ensuring that the classroom talk is about the subject matter and that it is not off-task talk. Consequently, this discussion of developing social interaction in the classroom, which is based upon the research evidence and theories previously described, requires some discussion of behaviour management strategies. However, the focus of the work is on building the

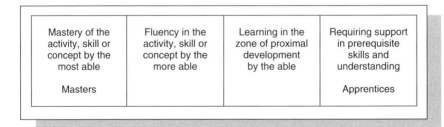

Figure 4.1 Classifying learners to promote cognitive apprenticeship using peer masters

social classroom and, as such, is based upon the classic classroom assumption that simply promoting and allowing on-task talk will push out or suppress inappropriate off-task talk.

There are different forms of social interaction that we can promote which lead to enhanced learning:

- cognitive apprenticeships where the relationship is asymmetric with the learner receiving advice/support from a peer or teacher;
- collaborative working towards a common goal with learners sharing responsibilities;
- cooperative working towards individual goals but supporting and accommodating other learners;
- instructional teaching where the learner receives general advice through a personalised medium;
- pastoral support where the discussion focuses upon the social and emotional aspects of learning.

As we have seen in Chapter 2, aspects of cooperation and cooperative activity can be classified as cognitive or physical. The cognitive helping activities include doing (skills), showing (skills), telling (knowledge) and explaining (understanding). The sharing activities include loaning, giving, hiring (i.e. loaning for a return) and taking turns.

The dialogues within the physical situations relate to accepted classroom mores of interaction or manners. It is important that the teacher promotes language and conduct in line with the school ethos through example of his or her behaviour, instruction to the learners or interceding in discussions. This can be at the level of reminding of "please and thank you" and encouraging the appropriate phatic (i.e. performing a social task) discourse.

The dialogues associated with the cognitive aspects of cooperation focus on learning outcomes; they reflect the degree to which the learners are engaged with the subject matter. Teachers can raise that level of engagement by making explicit some of the learning outcomes that they wish to achieve. A strategy devised by Shirley Clarke used the acronyms WALT, WILF and TIB (Clarke, 2001; see Figure 4.2).

Traditional or physical cooperation is reflected in the sharing of classroom resources. A learner also possesses other resources: their knowledge, understanding and skills. Cooperation is also reflected in how they are shared or communicated in a positive way to another. A learner shares his or her skills by doing or showing (i.e. helping); a learner shares his or her knowledge by telling; and a learner shares his or her understanding by explaining.

WALT	We are learning to ...	Also known as learning objectives, these are explicit statements of the skills and understanding that will occur during the lesson.
WILF	What I'm looking for ...	Also known as learning outcomes, these are the observable or assessable outcomes of the learning activities. Making these statements explicit supports teacher assessment, self-assessment and peer assessment.
TIB	That is because ...	Also known as the rationale for learning, this helps learners to identify alternative routes to achieving the learning outcomes.

Figure 4.2 WALT, WILF and TIB
Source: Adapted from Clarke, 2001

As we have seen in Chapter 2, cooperation and collaboration in the classroom are distinctly different phenomena, but they are inextricably connected. However, the heart of collaboration is the single goal being pursued by two or more learners. Collaboration leads to a single product that is achieved, and owned, by all the participants. That product can be a learning outcome, but learning is frequently tokenised in the classroom as a physical artefact that the group produces.

Collaboration is associated with group work and team work. Promoting collaboration and utilising the positive learning outcomes of collaboration means adopting the principles and strategies of good practice in those areas.

This model for promoting collaboration in the social classroom is orientated around teacher activity and classroom management. Collaboration is achieved through positive teacher action towards establishing groups and teams, setting learning outcomes that are more easily achieved through collaboration, encouraging informal collaboration and supporting or establishing collaboration when it does not occur naturally. Establishing good groups requires both an understanding and use of group mechanics by the teacher and the development of the learners' group work skills, knowledge and attitudes. Figure 4.3 identifies the key skills, knowledge, understandings and attitudes that learners should possess if they are to effectively contribute to group work.

	Resources	Curriculum	Structures
Learners' skills	Knowing how to use the resources (e.g. scissors, specific software, information sources, etc.)	Possessing the prerequisite experience to place them in the zone of proximal development.	Being able to fulfil the role by having the necessary skills for the role expected of them.
Learners' knowledge	Knowing what resources are available.	Knowing the goals, outcomes or success criteria of the activity (WALT and WILF).	Knowing what role they have within the group and the responsibilities they have for the activity.
Learners' understanding	Understanding concepts of suitability, efficiency and appropriateness with regard to choosing resources.	Understanding the rationale for the activity (TIB).	Understanding roles and responsibilities within group work.
Learners' attitudes	Respecting property and readiness to share, loan and hire resources.	Wanting to learn and being motivated by the subject matter.	Wanting to participate and contribute to the group.

Figure 4.3 Aspects of group work

Establishing teams within the classroom environment is based on the principles of group work except that there is the element of intergroup relationships. In conventional group work, we would like to see cooperation between groups. In teamwork, cooperation is replaced or enhanced by competition. The cooperative activities of sharing, loaning, hiring and selling may move distinctly to the latter, hiring and selling with strategic gain being made by the acquisition and disposal of particular resources. Competition in a fair situation would require the outcomes or success criteria for all teams to be the same; the teacher does not have the same freedoms to change the outcomes to meet the needs of a particular group.

Competition gives a range of benefits, including enhanced motivation (particularly towards ensuring completion), speed of activity and focused outcomes. It encourages leadership and the subsequent differentiation of roles within the team. It also encourages strategic thinking and enhances collaboration. Discussions may become more heated because of the competitive element; competition therefore provides opportunities to develop enhanced social skills. Competition may also provide opportunities to discuss the moral and ethical issues arising from spying and sabotage.

Competition is not always accepted as an appropriate feature of the classroom. With competition there are winners and losers; to compete means to "strive to gain or win something by defeating or establishing superiority over others" (Oxford University Press, 2009). Teachers' responsibility for the vulnerable means that we may be reluctant to set them up for losing. In this world, for the most part, participation in competition is voluntary and self-imposed. Rather, we collaborate with those we come into contact with, including our neighbours, relatives, colleagues and friends. It is perhaps not appropriate to impose a competitive ethos in the area of learning. Competition can lead the teams to focus on winning and not the learning; this is a serious criticism and all teachers need to be sensitive when setting up competitive situations.

The social classroom is characterised by periods of learning where learners are working individually or in small groups and frequently, but not necessarily continually, talking about the learning activity in a quiet way. In a successful collaborative social classroom, the following would not be seen:

- groups of learners chatting off-task;
- learners doing nothing or doing something inappropriate;
- learners sitting with their hands up, waiting for the attention of the teacher;
- learners working in total silence (see below).

The following activities encourage collaboration:

- assigning names to groups (i.e. giving a sense of identity and responsibility);
- celebrating a learner's achievements as a member of a group (e.g. Work of Sally Jones (Emerald group));
- creating a group noticeboard/display area (i.e. promoting identity and highlighting achievement);
- duties and tasks (e.g. scheduling or directing one person per group for each activity such as collecting resources, handing in work, etc.);
- physically dividing the class (e.g. arranging tables so that they form four, five or six groups);
- seating plan (i.e. consistency of location is maintained and activities completed jointly in the previous lesson can be continued);
- starters (i.e. setting short activities that can be or should be completed in pairs).

Through these activities, interdependence between members of the group can foster a group ethos and the required cooperation can form the basis for more formal and sustained collaboration. Collaboration can also be encouraged through informal actions of the teacher. The teacher offering rewards to all the members of collaborative groups can encourage group participation, for example, "David's group did very well last week; I will sign your merit cards now." It is particularly important to support or establish collaboration when it does not occur naturally. This can be done by direct intervention on an individual level by introducing two pupils and saying "work together because. . .". The reason may be that they have a common interest or focus of their work, they are socially excluded – forming a strong pair is the first step towards joining a group – or one of the pair requires the steadying influence of the other to ensure he or she remains on task or achieves the learning outcomes.

Supporting individuals through social interaction

It is a responsibility that the educational needs of all pupils are met through the classroom activities wherever possible. In many cases, a social classroom provides more support for individuals. For example, peer support is a natural part of the social classroom and pupils who become stuck can more readily seek advice and support from others. However, a social classroom can be a difficult place to work for pupils with some needs. For example, a child with attention difficulties may find the social interactions much more difficult to handle than a classroom with no such distractions. Managing pupils with special educational needs and managing a social classroom has both affordances and challenges.

Arising from earlier discussion in Chapter 2, we saw the importance of social interaction and the social and emotional aspects of learning. A major work in this field which underpins many of the UK strategies identifies the importance of the holistic approach. That is, dealing with the social and emotional needs of individuals can be achieved by working with the whole class, school or education authority. "It is less stigmatising to work with everyone, which means that those with problems are more likely to use the services offered and feel positive about them than if they feel they are being singled out" (Weare and Gray, 2003).

The pedagogy arising from the consideration of cooperation in the social classroom can be summarised as a number of principles of teacher actions. Teachers should:

- encourage cooperation and collaboration through action, instructions and advice;
- identify a code of conduct or classroom rules regarding talking and learners' behaviour in general;
- identify the affordances and challenges of competitive working within each text they teach;
- identify the group work skills, knowledge, understanding and attitudes that the learners need to develop to enable them to contribute as fully as possible;
- make the learning objectives and outcomes clear through a systematic and consistent approach (e.g. WALT and WILF) and make the rationale for the subject content clear;
- support the social and emotional development of learners through the whole-class and group discussions.

The social constructivist teacher must be aware of the values of co-operative interactions in the classroom and the implications for peer support and social development.

Summary

- Andragogy and cybergogy are key partners with pedagogy and our under-standing of the teaching processes.
- Being prepared for learning, both in a cognitive and an emotional sense, is important.
- When planning teaching, both structuring and sequencing learning, and providing alternative opportunities, should be considered.
- Cognitive apprenticeship leads to contextualised learning and collaboration.
- Social interaction has to be planned for and fostered.

Activities

- Consider, in the light of the content of this chapter, the important aspects of the constructivist pedagogy and how they could be translated into teaching strategies.

- Compare and contrast these aspects of pedagogy: collaboration and competition; cognitive apprenticeships and small group working; structure/ sequence and social interaction.

5

Strategies

By the end of this chapter you will be able to:

■ make informed choices about the selection of particular pedagogic approaches to classroom activities.

And you will have:

■ reflected on the scenarios presented in the light of the preceding chapters and in the light of commentaries.

> From the social constructivist perspective, the instructor – contrary to some misguided constructivist views – remains a pivotal classroom figure by creating activities that direct students toward subject mastery and that promote a certain level of cultural assimilation.
>
> (Hyslop-Margison and Strobel, 2008: 72)

Based on the underlying principles of the social aspects of constructivism and learning which we have considered in detail earlier, there emerges a set of strategies which can be identified and which are used by teachers in learning situations. We do not always knowingly design a learning activity which is based on the underlying principles; we do the planning by instinct and from a standpoint of experience of what we know works well. However, many teachers do look to socially engaging ways of encouraging learning. In this chapter we will consider some of these strategies and give some illustrations of the strategies in practice.

Strategies of a constructivist teacher

This section will outline some of the approaches taken by teachers who are positive about encouraging aspects of social learning with the classes that they teach. These teachers realise that providing opportunities for social interaction and dialogue, in one or more of their many guises, is an effective and productive way for them to plan and teach.

In a so-called "constructivist" classroom, some or all of the following approaches to encouraging learning will be evident:

- The teacher will encourage learner autonomy and initiative.
- The teacher will make use of primary sources and physical materials.
- The teacher will take into account the responses of the learners and make use of them to move learning on.
- The teacher will find out about learners' understanding of new ideas in advance of teaching about them.
- The teacher will encourage learners to engage in dialogue with both the teacher and each other.
- The teachers will encourage learners to think and enquire by asking thoughtful, open-ended questions and encouraging them to ask questions of each other.
- The teacher will seek elaboration of learners' responses.
- The teacher will engage learners in experiences that might bring about contradictions and then encourage discussion.

(Based on Brookes and Brookes, 1993)

All of the above, and other approaches, since the list is far from exhaustive, have the intention of assisting in the process of learning which is based on the constructivist premise that learning is an individual process which entails the personal construction of knowledge and understanding, which is built on a foundation of prior experience.

A teacher who values the principles of social constructivist and social learning theory will also make use of the approaches outlined above. The teacher is also very likely to use other approaches too, all of which will encapsulate one or more of the precepts detailed in Chapter 4.

Bearing in mind that any individual teacher is likely to use a range of different approaches to encourage learning – something that we will return to later in this chapter – the following activities, or approaches to organising learning activities in classrooms, will be evident when a teacher has a bias towards directing learning in a socially mediated way:

- a range of different dialogues will be employed, including in situations when traditionally work would be solitary and therefore "quiet";
- prior knowledge will be explored;
- learners will work on a shared task in pairs or other groupings;
- learners will explain what they have done;
- able/less able working and talking together;
- children will demonstrate a (physical) skill;
- children will explain how to do something (e.g. maths problem);
- teachers will ask questions;
- teachers will set open-ended tasks;
- scaffolding in all of its manifestations;
- models and modelling techniques will be used;
- homework being set which encourages/demands interaction with others (e.g. homework with talking, particularly practical activity, etc.).

Also, in teaching situations which are planned and mediated through a social learning perspective, the classrooms will be characterised, in general, by an absence of:

- learning by rote;
- working in silence (most of the time);
- "telling" learners points of fact or information with the expectation that it will be learned;
- undertaking whole pages of practice sums or language exercises.

Below is a series of vignettes set in classrooms or other learning contexts. Each of them illustrates at least one – often more than one – of the situations which a teacher has chosen to set up, with social learning in mind, in order to help the learners in each case achieve the learning outcomes set for the teaching.

Vignette 1: activating prior knowledge

In this vignette the learners are introduced to the use of a KWL grid. Working in pairs, the pupils identify "what I Know; what I Want to find out; what I have Learned".

In a class of 30 ten- and eleven-year-olds the teacher was about to begin a new topic on the history of transport. This particular topic was part of a wider look at Victorian Britain (see QCA, 2009).

As an experiment and with a view to helping the class to prepare for the work, the teacher wanted to make use of a KWL grid. This was something that she had been introduced to during an in-service training session dealing with information handling and it was based firmly in the constructivist/social constructivist arena. The teacher did not speak of the theoretical background to what she was doing, just the efficacy of using the grid as a means of helping the class to establish a starting point for the work and for focusing on specific research targets.

A KWL grid (what I Know; what I Want to find out; what I have Learned) is a device which helps pupils to consider a topic in a general, almost brainstorming way, and requires them to focus on specific questions which they would like to answer. By doing this it is likely that any browsing of information sources will be focused and therefore more likely to bear fruit. (For more information about KWL grids and their use, see Ogle, 1989 and Wray and Lewis, 1997.)

What I Know	What I Want to find out	What I have Learned
1. Polar bears, penguins and walruses live in the very cold parts of the world. 2. Penguins can't fly. 3. Emperor penguins are the biggest penguins.	1. What other animals live there? 2. Do they all fight or do they get on with each other? 3. Can they all swim? 4. Are there different sorts of polar bears?	1. Sea lions and seals. Different sorts of birds. 2. Penguins only live at the South Pole and polar bears only live at the North Pole and so they never meet each other. 3. Polar bears are good swimmers. 4. There is only one main type of polar bear. There are lots of different sorts of penguins.

Figure 5.1 What I Know; what I Want to find out; what I have Learned (KWL) grid

The teacher introduced the topic by saying that they were going to find out where something that they almost all used from time to time came from, who invented it and what the original ones were like. She asked the class to suggest what it might be that they would be studying. This seemed to be taking a long time, so she gave clues by miming riding a bicycle and the topic was then established. She asked for a show of hands in answer to a few introductory questions: "Who has a bike?"; "Who has ridden their bike in the last week?"; "What do we call a bike with three wheels/one wheel?"

She then set the first task, which involved working in pairs and making a first attempt at completing a KWL grid. The use of the grid was not wholly new to the class; they had been introduced to the notion in the previous term when starting a science topic. The plan was to jointly discuss and decide three items each for the "what I Know" column – this was to be renamed "what we Know" – and to think about formulating three questions for the second column.

The class set about this with enthusiasm. After a fairly short period, about five minutes, the teacher called the class together to review what had been done so far. Her plan was to share the many different items of knowledge from each pair with the class, then allow more time for the pairs to rethink their initial "what we Know" statements in the light of the class's contributions and revise the questions for which they wanted to seek out answers.

With the use of an electronic flipchart through the medium of an electronic whiteboard, the teacher made notes in the form of short headings to record the contributions of each of the pairs.

The process of sharing took a long time and this is because the teacher, at every stage, allowed time for additional discussion and for the class to challenge any statements of fact that they were either unsure about or with which they disagreed. An example of this is the statement made by one of the pairs to the effect that the penny-farthing was the first bike. This was immediately challenged by a boy who had as one of his facts that the one-wheeled bike was the first example of wheeled transport in history. After some noisy contributions from many in the class, the teacher calmed them down, asked if anyone knew for certain that one of the two examples given was not the first and suggested that it had become an important question for research. She allowed the two pairs in the disagreement to use this for one of their "Want to find out" questions, made it clear that they would be reporting back to the class at a later stage and moved on with the collection of facts. There were some other contributions that led to a measure of disagreement, and these were dealt with in a similar way. Only one child was aware that James Starley, who has been attributed with contributing a great deal to the early development of the bicycle, had actually lived and worked in the city in which the school was located (Coventry).

The class was set to work on the final versions of their KWL grids, this time on a copied sheet, rather than on a page of their working books. The buzz of conversation was loud, but when observing it was clear that all, as far as it was possible to tell, of the conversation was related to the task in hand. Some strayed off a little with tales of bicycling exploits, but in general there was a good deal of dialogue in pairs, sometimes with minor interventions from the teacher. At the end of the lesson in a short plenary it was clear that the task had been completed, previous knowledge and experience had been dredged and activated and the class was well primed for taking on the next phase of the work, namely seeking answers to their questions.

Commentary

The strategy employed here which is designed to activate prior knowledge is commonly employed by teachers. Often it is something which is done instinctively, sometimes quite swiftly as a reminder and sometimes at greater length with more detailed attention paid to ensuring that both individuals and the group as a whole have explored their shared understanding and knowledge of a given topic. In terms of schema theory (Bartlett, 1958; Johnson-Laird, 1983), the way that a new topic can be introduced by allowing time for the learners to reflect on what they already know and understand is referred to as activating schemas. The idea is that a notional schema is to be operated upon by learning tasks and activities, and if Piaget's notions of assimilation and accommodation (see Woolfolk, 1993 for a review of this aspect of Piaget's work) are to take place in a straightforward way, then the individual's schema should be called to the fore and revisited. In short, the schema should be activated and made ready for use.

What sets the learning activities within the realm of social constructed learning is the emphasis placed upon working with another. The use of the

KWL grid is an ideal mechanism for, first, activating prior knowledge and, second, encouraging focus on specific aspects of a topic to research further by the opportunity to talk, discuss and explain to one another, in pairs, and then to a larger group, to the teacher and to the class. Certainly, it would have been possible for the teacher to ask the group to work individually on the grids, but this would have excluded the opportunities which arise from being able to listen to another's ideas and experiences, moving memories into action and ideas and recalling facts. In short, the opportunity to work collaboratively opens up a range of possibilities which would not otherwise be available to learners or their teacher.

Vignette 2: computer-mediated collaboration

In this example of social constructivism in practice the learners communicate through a conventional online chat room.

In this example of social learning in practice we will see a teacher encouraging social interaction and dialogue between learners relating to website evaluation. The work is carried out by making use of online websites to be evaluated. The next stage requires the use of computer-mediated dialogue via the medium of a closed, and therefore safe, chat room.

The work took place with a group of higher ability mixed-gender Year Nine pupils in a large urban secondary school. For the teacher it was a development of work that had previously been carried out without the use of a chat room and, in the view of the teacher, with limited success. The context of the work was in an English and media module relating to both evaluating sources of information and writing for an audience. The group had used the chat room approach previously as a way of exploring the differences between formal and informal writing. The group as a whole was well versed in the use of technology over a very wide range of applications. The group knew each other well and had a reputation for mutual support and an enthusiasm for working with computers.

The group was asked to visit preassigned websites, explore the content and structure and evaluate the quality in terms of appearance, navigation, content validity and accessibility in relation to a particular audience – in this case a class of younger children working on a history project. The teacher's previous experience of website evaluation with similar groups was that each pupil worked independently; even when asked to work in pairs, they each used their own computer and made their own notes. The aim of the activity was to move the pupils from making simple descriptive statements to making evaluative statements that included judgements with supporting evidence. As a result, the teacher hoped that there would be an increase in understanding of the evaluation process. This is a good example of using technology-mediated activities in order to work towards achieving learning outcomes in a domain other than technology.

The students were individually subscribed to a private (bounded) chat room where only they and their teacher could read or write comments. The first messages in the chat room were sent by the teacher, as preparation, prior to the lesson. These initial messages described the activity and then provided the addresses of the websites to be evaluated. The teacher considered that there was no need for a formal introduction to the lesson since it had been described in detail at the end of the previous lesson and also because the lesson was short and time was at a premium. The group entered the classroom, logged on and entered the chat room.

Some students did not immediately understand the problem, but others were able to give support by answering their questions in an informal way. (This is the first example of a social dimension to the work. It was not planned, but happened, as these things do, spontaneously.) The teacher considered that there was not necessarily a need for intervention unless it became obvious that any misinformation was being given or any misconceptions arose and remained unresolved.

After an initial period of talk and interaction between the pairs, the group settled to work reasonably quietly, but with obvious low-level talk which appeared to be wholly task-related.

The time soon came when comments were to be sent to the chat room concerning the individual websites. As each pair sent their agreed comments, the teacher was able to make comments in reply which were designed to encourage the pairs to refine their views and comments and eventually develop a well-balanced and objective review of the site in question. The site would have to be written in a style and register suitable for the younger audience. Initially the comments were focused on the content and appearance of the websites.

The teacher was keen to generate a dialogue between himself and the contributors. If, for example the contributions were thin or unfocused, the teacher chose to employ a flaming strategy, that is, sending a message intended to provoke an immediate response by being critical or even dismissive of the original contribution. The initial exchanges were, to an extent, social in nature and not focused on the aims of the lesson. The teacher was able to positively reinforce appropriate responses with short comments praising the comment or the style of the comment. This had the effect of generating better and properly focused conversation.

After a short period, different conversations or threads appeared in the chat room. These were mostly in relation to a specific website and those working on the same sites concentrated on responding and contributing to the thread related to what they were doing and ignoring the others. This worked well as the smaller groupings looking at a specific site were able to discuss, in the chat room, the features of the site while developing a critical, rather than descriptive, response to it. As the lesson developed, it was clear that many comments sent to the chat room were being ignored since they were not directly pertinent to their interest, but subgroups in the class continued to contribute and discuss each of the sites in turn.

The teacher took on the role of identifying and making the threads explicit, drawing threads together, sometimes amalgamating threads and, in a couple of cases, closing a thread down when it was duplicating what was being done elsewhere or if it seemed not to be meeting the aims of the lesson.

The teacher also spent a little time modelling good evaluative practice. By doing this, the teacher encouraged an approach to evaluation which was picked up by the contributors. In some cases the teacher wrote direct comments, such as "Give an example of what you mean here" or similar, designed to improve the final website evaluations.

Towards the end of the discussion period the teacher asked individuals to put up a summary relating to one aspect of the evaluation. The others in the group were asked to respond to each summary. This was actually continued in the next lesson as a change to the original plan because it began to become a valuable sharing opportunity and a chance for more comment and feedback to contribute to the finished products.

At the end of the second lesson the teacher spent time drawing together, on a big screen, the different threads of comment. The teacher specifically drew attention to the more detailed and constructive evaluations which had been posted. Having a break between lessons actually gave the teacher more time to sift through the contributions to the chat room and pick out those which exemplified what was being looked for.

In an informal discussion after the two lessons the teacher talked about the success of the work. He strongly believed that the most important final outcome of the work was not a set of website evaluations for use elsewhere, but a shared, socially constructed understanding of the evaluation process and the ways in which language can be used to provide appropriate material for specific audiences.

Commentary

This vignette illustrates a range of approaches to teaching that fall within the realm of supporting social learning. It also illustrates that discussion need not be entirely of the face-to-face variety. Dialogue mediated through technology over large distances can be as effective (Barak and Block, 2006; Bernard et al., 2004; Danet et al., 1995; Freiermuth and Jarrell, 2006; Grigsby, 2001; Kordaki, 2005; Richards, 2003) as sitting together and working through a task collaboratively. Obviously, in this vignette, the contributors to the chat room were actually sitting in the same room as each other, and some would argue that they might just as well have organised themselves differently and spoken as a group. This may well be true, but there is no doubt that the volume of written output and of relevant contributions made as a result of using the chat room was far greater than might have been expected from a more usual classroom-based approach to the same work.

This description is a strong example of the importance of the teacher. As we saw in the quote at the start of this chapter, the role of the teacher (instructor) is crucial; the planning, preparation and active participation of the teacher were all essential to the success of the work. Too often it is possible to allow work to proceed without any intervention or feedback of any sort. The only notion of how good an individual's work might be can sometimes be a grade and a comment on returned work. In this case, there was a continuous stream of feedback and interaction that contributed to the developing threads of chat comments. The chat room is an effective way in which informal learning can be fostered (Willett and Sefton-Green, 2003). The other way in which the teacher was crucial, both to individuals and then to the group as a whole, was in the way that contributions were modelled; there were real and developing examples of what a good evaluation might contain and finally look like.

The teacher was modelling, pointing out aspects of contributions to the chat by the group members which met the criteria for an effective and useful evaluation. The group as a whole was responding to the models presented in the way that is described by the apprenticeship description of learning (Bandura, 1997a and 1997b; Lave, 1988). Clearly, there was more going on than simple observation and imitation, but in some cases a contribution to a thread could be seen as being based on a model contribution presented by the teacher. Indeed, in some cases it seemed that a style of writing was used based on a model provided by another member of the class.

Vignette 3: working in pairs

This vignette illustrates the affordances of working in pairs, encouraging discussion and disagreement – social interaction and dialogue with a peer.

Based on experience in the previous school year and a continuing professional development (CPD) session covering the use of pupil collaboration on tasks often seen as being individual in nature, a teacher altered her approach to some geography-based work. The work involved looking at places and other major geographical features around the world, identifying them with the use of an atlas and completing sets of world and more local maps with appropriate labels. The work was with a mixed ability, mixed gender class of 28 in a rural primary school.

Having returned to teaching the previous year and being dismayed by the children's apparent lack of knowledge and interest in the names and locations of cities, countries, rivers, mountain ranges and other notable world features, she sought out a set of books, *Find a Place in the British Isles* and *Find a Place in the World*, that she had used some years before in a previous school. Unable to track down copies of the

---

book and following encouragement to make wider use of information and communication technology (ICT) she found, with help, a selection of websites which allowed for very similar exploration and exercises to those originally found in the books. She felt a little uncomfortable with the use of ICT but made good use of what was available. There were two computers available in the classroom and a bank of six in a shared area which could be used by negotiation with other teachers.

She introduced the class to the sites and what needed to be done and set them off individually to work through a series of tasks which involved labelling and otherwise identifying and naming a range of different national and international features, including countries, counties (in the UK), rivers, lakes and mountain ranges. Although the teacher's plan was for individual work, there was inevitably some talk which took place between those undertaking the work. The teacher was happy to allow this and reflected that it was in line with ideas of collaboration and discussion to which she had been introduced at the CPD session. At the time she did not fully realise the potential for discussion and collaborative work and the way that encouraging working in pairs would transform both the enthusiasm for learning and the eventual learning outcomes.

During the course of the term, when this work was being undertaken, she found that enthusiasm for the work increased. On many occasions, such as wet playtimes and before school, children were choosing to use the websites and, invariably, working in pairs and small groups. She noticed that the quality of talk around the computers at these times was, in some cases, at what she considered to be a very sophisticated level:

Child A: "I know that the Indus is in India, but so is the . . . er . . . Ganges, look at the shape of it here [in the atlas] it bends right round."

Child B: "Could be . . . I'm not sure . . . check in the bigger book [atlas] . . . does it change to go east or west?"

Child A: "East . . . no west . . . I don't know . . . get the big book."

As the term progressed, the teacher altered the way in which the work was undertaken. There were two computers in the room and so this work was not undertaken as a class activity, but as an activity completed in turns during different times of the day. She hoped that by providing the opportunity for work in pairs she would encourage the high level of talk, disagreement, negotiation and eventual resolution leading to satisfaction and, most importantly for her, new learning that she had observed during the informal use of the activities in break times. This was the case. There was a far greater level of enjoyment in the work, greater engagement with the content and the use of the reference books which were available and, by both formal and informal measures, a high level of learning.

Websites used:

http://www.mape.org.uk/startower/world/resources/broken.htm
http://www.nwlg.org/pages/resources/mapgames/geog.html
http://www.mape.org.uk/startower/world/index.htm

Commentary

This example of encouraging joint tasks based on discussion is a good example of how a seemingly mundane exercise, which the class was not particularly enthusiastic about initially, became something which generated excitement, generated an enthusiasm for work and for success and led to clear learning gains in terms of the desired learning outcomes set by the teacher.

The teacher was initially reluctant to allow for work in pairs. This lack of enthusiasm was based on the view that collaborative work has less value than individual work and can in some ways be seen as cheating (see Williams, 1999 for an interesting view on this). This view had dissipated by the time the teacher had spent a term encouraging collaboration and discussion and initiating a way of work that, even though advocated by the trainers in the CPD session, had been introduced by the children themselves out of normal classroom hours.

The discussion about the work and the semi-collaborative nature of the work as it progressed came about, in part, because the two classroom computers were next to each other and the teacher set the individuals to work on the same exercise at the same time; it also happened because there is a natural propensity to talk about what we are doing, especially if it is perceived that someone else is engaged in the same work. We know from the work of Vygotsky and others that talk is a medium for learning which has to be taken seriously. Fisher and Larkin (2005) present a picture of children who "love to talk and who talk confidently and enthusiastically with their peers but who recognise clearly that teachers, and to a lesser extent other adults, control when and how they talk in school" (13). In this study, the children overwhelmingly came across as eager to talk whether about their work or any other topic: " . . . impression was that the children love to talk and talk about anything and everything" (13). Many of us know from experience that this is the case and, with social learning in mind, we can recognise that to channel children's talk towards the focus of the work to be completed can only serve to enhance learning.

Initially, in this vignette, the teacher confessed a cynicism towards the value of children working together in this way and had not been convinced by the CPD input. This view was reversed during the course of the term.

Vignette 4: adults learning about teaching

In this vignette the apprenticeship model is illustrated by a group of adults learning about the processes of teaching using programmable toys. It also exemplifies the value of legitimate peripheral participation.

This example of how Bandura sees learning by social means, and by the apprenticeship model, was observed in a group of adults following a Foundation Degree module on a degree programme leading to a qualification in Early Childhood Studies. It was concerned with children's learning and the use of ICT.

The group was made up of 20 female students following a Foundation Degree programme for Higher Level Teaching Assistant competence. All of them worked in an Early Years setting of one sort or another, some in nurseries, some in a more formal school setting and some in a range of other care or support situations. The ages of the students ranged from 22 to 43. The group had widely different experience of using ICT, either for themselves or with children. Some had previously worked in situations rich with computer use (e.g. banks, medical clerical work), others had no experience at all of using computers except in the context of the module that they were following. Those with few skills were on a steep learning curve as assessed work for the course on which they were enrolled had to be submitted electronically and therefore word processed and there was a commitment to use online resources in teaching sessions and for follow-up tasks.

The focus of the session was on the use of peripheral and related artefacts such as programmable toys, digital cameras, microscopes and movie cameras. The session, after an introduction explaining the context, was designated as practical. A series of tasks were set. They would be completed with a minimum level of support and no instructions were given concerning how to operate any of the devices to be used. The reason for this was to illustrate the possibilities for learning in groups where there is a variety of levels of experience and expertise with some of the devices and where dialogue, discussion and observation might have an important role.

The task which is the focus of this vignette was to be carried out by a group of six students who were chosen randomly from the whole group. Two other groups were given the same task.

The task required the group to choreograph a short, synchronised dance sequence with three Bee-Bots. A Bee-Bot is a programmable toy which is fairly widely used: "Bee-Bots are programmable floor robots aimed at the Early Years and Key Stage 1" (Kent, 2004). Bee-Bots and other programmable toys enable young children to learn through play about control, directional language and a good deal more. The Bee-Bot is the right size for small hands and has been designed to be intuitive and easy to use. The child has simply to program the toy to move forwards, backwards and turn left or right by pressing the large arrow buttons on its back. It will move accurately in 15-centimetre steps. It is able to store and recall up to 40 steps (see TTS, 2009).

Within the group there was one member who had some limited experience of using a Bee-Bot with children, one member who had seen one in use and the remaining group members had no experience at all of Bee-Bot or any other similar device.

In the context of this activity there was a certain reluctance on the part of the whole group, including those with some experience, to take any sort of control and make a start with completing the task. Gradually, those with a little knowledge did take the lead and there began a short time of tentative experimentation when one or two of the group demonstrated the little that they knew, giving a rudimentary commentary of what they were doing while the other group members stood well back. The body language of those with no experience and their lack of participation in this initial phase of the group work was interesting. Since the Bee-Bots were being used on the floor, those operating them at first were kneeling or sitting; those not taking part remained standing with arms folded, keeping a respectful distance between themselves and the action that was unfolding on the carpet. They were in fact keeping very much to the periphery (Bandura, 1977; Lave and Wenger, 1991) of the activity, but they were taking an interest in what was being done and said by those with a little more know-how.

What followed was actually quite remarkable. Bandura's model of social learning refers to legitimate peripheral participation (see Chapter 1). If an attempt were made to visualise this phenomenon, it is quite likely that the physical arrangement of the students in this group, the observations and comments made and the responses of those with a measure of expertise would be very close to the visualisation.

The task was, little by little, completed. Those operating (i.e. programming) the Bee-Bots worked and experimented together (in a highly socially constructivist manner), while those with no experience demonstrated a lack of confidence but a great interest in what was being undertaken on behalf of the group. After a short time of trial and error and with a certain amount of success, the task was more or less complete and the time soon came when the end product, the synchronised dance routine, was to be shared with the whole group. At this stage some of the peripheral participants chose to experiment for themselves. There were other Bee-Bots available and not in use by the whole group. In pairs and singly, those who were totally new to the very notion of programming and using the Bee-Bots began to experiment and develop an understanding of the ways in which a structured sequence could be built and a specific task answered. Initially, attempts were made to program the Bee-Bot to go a certain distance and then return. This being accomplished, slightly more expansive targets were set and, in turn, accomplished. Within the space of 20 minutes (about 15 minutes as observers), the novices were able to create and put into practice simple yet challenging routines. With a little more time, they would have been able to answer the initial task set to the whole group.

Commentary

This is a simple yet clear illustration of the way in which social learning theory describes the process which is undertaken in a range of both formal and informal situations where novices observe and in other ways engage with more expert practitioners and in so doing prepare themselves for beginning and then developing particular skills. The two terms which aptly describe the situation in the vignette – "apprenticeship model" and "legitimate peripheral participation" (Bandura, 1977; Lave and Wenger, 1991) – are used to describe models of learning which rely on a relationship between experts and novices. The relationships in situations where learning is progressing in the ways described by these two theoretical standpoints (which are very closely related) can vary enormously. The expert could be a master craftsman demonstrating how to undertake a complex skill in a complex domain, such as wiping a joint, which is a skill needed by accomplished plumbers:

> Joint-wiping is one of the ancient mysteries of the plumber's craft. It was maintained from time immemorial until modern times by the initiation of the apprentice by the master-craftsman into the skill and into the knowledge of the secrets of the peculiar alloy of lead and tin used for the process.
>
> (Innes, 1949: 275)

The point about this situation is that the novice observes as the master demonstrates. There may well be other interaction between the two (e.g. conversation, questions and answers). In some cases, the master could perhaps guide the hand of a novice; a tennis coach, for example, could hold the hand or arm of a beginner in order to show how a particular stroke should be made.

In the vignette, the novices were very clearly peripheral to the initial element of the activity. Not only were they only peripherally involved in that they were present, but made no contribution, but they physically placed themselves on the periphery of what was going on, standing back and observing almost as if to avoid drawing attention to themselves. It is possible to imagine this situation in a primitive social setting, and to consider it in this way might illustrate the process quite well. In a primitive setting, possibly in a tribal village, there are certain fairly crucial skills which need to be acquired by the youngest members of a group if they are to grow and develop into effective members of the group who contribute to the daily routine work of the group. Groups of this nature need to work together (e.g. when hunting) in order for the group to survive and prosper. Children will be in many situations where they observe adults carrying out certain tasks and undertaking particular duties. By being legitimately present and by participating, in a very small way at first, peripherally, but increasingly as they mature and are shown how to do certain things, they develop the skills necessary for them to become valuable adult members of the community (LeVine *et al.*, 1994). They develop the skills and understanding that are required for them to function safely and cooperatively in their particular social setting by increasingly participating in the daily routines of the group.

Vignette 5: collaborating to learn

Collaboration is a most effective means by which social constructivist-based learning can be established. In this example, pupils are learning how to keep the score in a volleyball match.

> This episode comes from a GCSE PE lesson with a new group of Year Ten pupils in which the finer detail of the scoring system of volleyball was being investigated. The teacher came to realise that a small proportion of the group was not able to work easily with the mechanics of the scoring and was keen to remedy this as soon as possible so that they could move on to the main task at hand, which was to compare the scoring systems of other court and net games and devise a uniform system which could be applied to a range of similar games.
>
> The action taken by the teacher was simple and involved pairing a confident scorer with a partner who was not able to operate the system. She gave them a video of a volleyball match and asked them to follow the game with the sound turned down and to jointly score the game.
>
> The teacher was able to leave the pairs alone while she covered another aspect of the planned work with the rest of the group. She did not monitor the progress of the scoring exercise but was gratified to see, in the next lesson, that those who had originally not been able to score a match were competent and able to both explain the system with reasonable accuracy and score a series of short trial games within the group.

She asked those who had been the novices how they had worked with the video. The account given was similar in all cases. They had been told by the expert how the system works and listened for a few minutes as the expert scored a section of the game by giving a running commentary and writing down the score on paper as the game progressed. The novice asked questions and attempted to keep a score at the same time, gradually joining in and making decisions about the awarding of points. After a short period, the expert stopped scoring out loud and the job passed on to the novice who soon became more or less proficient. Any mistakes made were challenged, some by the expert simply stating that it was wrong and giving the correct version and some by the expert asking if the novice scorer was "sure about that".

Commentary

Working with a partner in a relaxed atmosphere where one of the pair was an expert and the other a novice seemed to work extremely well in this case. There are similarities with the previous vignette in that we are looking at an expert/novice situation and the apprenticeship analogy holds good (Bandura 1977; Lave and Wenger, 1991). There was dialogue and the notion of peripheral participation involved. The novice was in the position of the apprentice who was able to observe and gradually join in with the task, making use of newly acquired knowledge and skills under the guidance of the expert (apprentice master). Within a relatively short period of time and with only limited practice, the system of scoring seemed to have been understood by the novice and to some extent internalised to the point where the novice was able to explain the system – which they could not do before the paired session – and also able to operate the scoring system in a real situation.

Scaffolded support was provided in this example by the peer expert. Progress was made based on a foundation of confused understanding of the rules of the game but a broader understanding of similar games and other scoring systems.

This approach might not always be successful. A part of the reason for success with this approach depends on the relationship within the pair. Teachers need to consider the composition of pairs and other groups carefully. In some cases, friendship grouping might be appropriate, but this is not always the case. In cases with a pair who do not know each other well or in which there is an imbalance between the pair in terms of expertise, confidence or charisma perceived by one or other member, there are possibilities of failure. In most cases the pairings or groupings need to be considered and monitored. Working in pairs and discussing authentic, meaningful tasks are characteristics of teaching based on social constructivism.

Vignette 6: cross-curriculum collaboration

In this vignette we see how learning is enhanced by bringing together students who view the same concepts from different perspectives and with different experiences. In the activity learners collaborate to meet common goals through social interaction, dialogue with a peer and focused tasks. In the commentary that follows, reflections are made about the characteristics of collaboration, promotive interaction, individual accountability and interpersonal skills.

Based on experience and study on a masters-level CPD course, the teacher wanted to encourage her students studying in two connected but contrasting fields (i.e. computer science and electronics) to support each other's understanding of common concepts through collaborative activities.

The teacher works at an 11–18 secondary school. The teacher teaches GCE computing and a colleague teaches GCE electronics. Although the conceptual elements of the curriculum are similar, they are taught and learned in different ways using different practical examples, different metaphors of explanation and different assessments of understanding.

Because the collaborative work cannot be timetabled during school time, the event was set up in out-of-school hours. The activity was planned and designed in such a way that the students would have to work together to solve problems and achieve a common goal. The activity incorporated no planned teacher intervention, although teachers were present for safety reasons.

The students had access to tools, software and previously tested desktop personal computers into which a known fault was introduced.

Students were set these objectives for the day: find and fix the introduced fault, dismantle the computer as far as possible, correctly rebuild it, install an operating system, connect some external control hardware and program it using the installed software.

Students were required to bring their own knowledge together in order to solve the problems presented to them. The electronics students were able to contribute knowledge concerning transistors, clocks and printed circuit boards. The computing students were able to contribute knowledge concerning installation of high-level devices and software. To accomplish the tasks they had to communicate effectively by questioning, answering and giving feedback to each other. In one instance, a student made a mistake with a component; another student identified the mistake and was able to provide correction. Bringing the two disciplines together was evident during a discussion of the heatsink. The computing students knew how it had to be installed and the electronics students knew its purpose, but its construction and material was successfully derived by discussion.

The success of the collaboration was aptly summed up by one student as ". . . you are able to learn from your peers on matters that you do not understand yourself."

Commentary

On reflection of the activity and considering the literature, the teacher identified five characteristics of collaboration: positive interdependence, promotive interaction, individual accountability, interpersonal skills and a common goal.

Positive interdependence

One group member cannot achieve success unless the others also achieve success (Falchikov 2001; Gillies, 2007). Efforts must be coordinated to ensure that all group members achieve specific individual goals that contribute to the group goal. This goal setting must be overt and obvious to the group to promote interdependence. Gillies (2007) argues that when working together towards a group goal, group members perceive themselves to be more interdependent than when working in competition or alone. This has an effect on how they interact with one another. Crook (2000), in *Rethinking*

Collaborative Learning, also identifies this interdependence as a motivation for dialogue between group members.

Promotive interaction

Once individual group members acknowledge that their own success depends on the success of the other members, the individuals should modify their behaviour. They make the connection between the common goal and the achievement of another's individual goal. Students must encourage and facilitate others' efforts by giving assistance, giving constructive feedback, engaging in dialogues and sharing resources to accomplish the goal (Gillies, 2007).

Individual accountability

While promotive interaction ensures that group members aid others to perform to the best of their abilities, individuals are also responsible for ensuring their own best performance. Group members have to accept responsibility for their own contributions to achieving the group goal (Gillies, 2007). Members can be motivated to better performance by the realisation that they are accountable to their peers for their own efforts in achieving the group goal. Falchikov (2001) asserts that individual account-ability has been achieved when all members take on the responsibility of doing a fair share of the work associated with achieving the common goal. Once group members have recognised their own accountability, they can better help the group towards the common goal.

Interpersonal skills

Listening, taking turns, sharing and giving constructive feedback form the basis for collaborative group work. Group members may not always possess these skills. Falchikov (2001) also emphasises the importance of developing these social skills, in her study of peer tutoring (see the description of Skillstreaming in Chapter 4).

Common goal

The actual type of task set for the collaborative work may not matter a great deal (Falchikov, 2001) as long as it has a goal towards which all members can work. According to Christiansen *et al.* (2003) in their work in the field of mathematics education, this goal may change during the collaboration. Even though in the beginning each member may believe he or she understands the common goal, it may be changed by the actual act of the collaboration itself. Regardless of the actual task or a changing goal, the task should afford opportunities for the demonstration of reasoning strategies, conflict management and active mutual involvement (Selby, 2009).

Vignette 7: paired game making

In this vignette we see how learning and creative activities can be fostered through collaborative work and how the pressures for curriculum success, from the pupils as much as the system, encourage a division of labour.

The setting is an 11–16 secondary school in the south of England where the successful ICT department is introducing computer programming into the curriculum through game design. The activity is also being monitored as part of a research programme related to the developing ICT curriculum.

In this example of paired working, a mixed ability group of pupils aged 13 to 14 years designed and developed a computer game, over a 16-hour unit of work, using Game Maker software (http://www.yoyogames.com/make). This program is accessible to beginners and allows more able pupils to create complex games. Users create graphic objects and add events and drag and drop actions to control them. A set of standard action libraries is available for movement, control structures, drawing, scoring and so on and a scripting language (GML) allows users to write code to extend the functionality of their games.

The work began by the group researching several online games before they began to plan their own. They played computer games which had been constructed in the software they were to use so that they could gain an idea of the potential and limitations of the program. They followed a series of screen-based video tutorials to build skills in the game authoring software before they began to design their own games. The game authoring process involves developing skills in constructing game narratives and understanding game mechanics, creating and manipulating graphics and sound assets and programming the game itself. It is an engaging, immersive and creative activity. It also allows pupils to make use of their prior learning in out-of-school contexts since many young people play computer games at home.

Pupils had had no prior experience in game authoring or in working in a pair on an extended project. They worked in pairs to research, plan, design, implement and test a computer game suitable for a younger age group. Pupils agreed that working as a pair was a predominantly positive experience; each viewed the other as a supportive and significant learning partner. An interesting outcome of the paired work was that some pairs tended to split tasks and work individually on different aspects of the game so that they were not working together and not generating any voice data. They considered that it was more efficient and quicker to split tasks in this way. Although they claimed that they were working together, what they meant was that they were working on a common product. The actual instances when both partners were engaged in solving the same problem together on the same computer occurred mainly with the programming elements and did not occur as frequently as envisaged. The notion of ownership was quite strongly felt by some pairs; it was their game and they did not like the teacher imposing restrictions, such as "There should be no violence" and "Characters and game narratives should be 'politically correct'." Some pairs viewed teacher intervention as an unwelcome interruption, such was their immersion in the activity.

Commentary

In this vignette it was seen how the process of creativity and learning to program were impacted upon by the requirement that the pupils had to work in pairs. Those effects were both positive and negative. It is clear that pupils need also be taught the skills and expectations relevant to collaborative work if they are to be successful in paired projects.

Working with a partner in a pressured, goal-orientated atmosphere seemed to force the pupils into a division of labour where each took responsibility for an aspect of the work. There are not the explicit or overarching similarities with the previous vignettes where an expert/novice situation is established (Bandura 1977; Lave and Wenger, 1991). However, it was noted that some dialogue involved the notion of peripheral participation where each partner kept a watching brief on the work of the other. This clearly exemplifies Vygotsky's description of the ZPD, which is the

> level of potential development as determined through problem solving . . . in collaboration with more capable peers . . . What children can do

with the assistance of others might be in some sense even more indicative of their mental development than what they can do alone.

(Vygotsky, 1978: 85)

Importantly, in the field of ICT, many of the working procedures of programming, systems design, consultancy and product development takes place in teams and collaboration skills are essential.

Vignette 8: coming to a joint conclusion

In this vignette we see how learning might be held back when certain conditions are not provided. In the commentary that follows, some suggestions are made, from the social learning perspective, which would likely improve the learning outcomes for the class involved.

In a science lesson considering air pressure, the teacher gave a demonstration that is often used to illustrate the effect of air pressure on a can which has had its internal pressure reduced.

The class were in Year Six and so aged 10 and 11. There were 13 boys and 15 girls. As far as the teacher knew, this was the first time that any work related to air pressure had been introduced to the class. In his initial introduction to the topic it became apparent that the class as a whole had virtually no discernable knowledge of the concept of pressure in general and of air pressure in particular.

The demonstration consisted of heating a small amount of water in a can similar to a five-litre metal oil can. Once the water in the can reached a fairly high temperature which was close to boiling, the can was removed from the heat source, immediately sealed with a screw cap and left to cool. As the water had been approaching boiling point, the air inside the can had also risen in temperature, expanded and escaped from the can through the open lid. The water had been hot enough for a good deal of it to have vaporised and filled the can with steam. Obviously some steam had also escaped through the open lid of the can. Had the can been left to cool naturally after the lid had been sealed, after some time, possibly as long as between five and ten minutes, the air inside the can would have cooled and reduced in

---

volume and the steam would have condensed and returned to being water. The volume of the steam would have been far greater than the volume of the water. The cooling of the air and the condensing of the steam together would result in a much smaller overall volume of gas in the sealed can and a reduction in the internal pressure. The external air pressure would then be greater than the internal pressure and the effect would be that the can would effectively be crushed by the force of pressure from outside.

If the teacher had left the can to cool on its own, all might well have gone according to plan. In the event, since time was short and the teacher felt that he should hurry the experiment along, he squirted cold water on the outside of the can through a flexible pipe attached to a tap. This speeded up the cooling process quite effectively.

Had the whole episode been allowed to take place without any water being sprayed on the can to speed the cooling process, there would have been no extraneous observations for the class. In the event, the extraneous observation of the can being soaked with water served to confuse the phenomenon which was supposed to have been demonstrated.

As the class watched, the cooling effect of the water had the desired effect and the can collapsed inwards with a fairly loud but short, metal-crunching sound. Without discussing the event, the teacher asked the class to return to their desks and sit in their usual discussion groups of three. He asked them to talk about what they had just seen and to try and explain why the can had collapsed in such a dramatic fashion. The teacher left the class to discuss the demonstration for five minutes and then asked for them to report back to the group with their explanations. To his dismay the first group suggested that the water sprayed on to the can had caused it to collapse because heating the can had softened the metal and made it susceptible to crushing from a relatively small and light amount of water.

In the vain hope that other groups in the class would be able to explain the event in a way more aligned with the reality of the situation, he did not comment, but asked the remaining groups to give their versions. All of the groups gave a similar account of what they had seen. In one case, the weakness of the can was likened to a wet, soggy paper bag which became weaker the wetter it became. The effect of the heat on the contents of the can was not considered by any of the groups reporting back.

Commentary

This is an example in which some of what we know about constructivist learning was ignored and in which the failure by the teacher to both prepare and then intervene appropriately caused a range of misconceptions to arise.

At the start of the new topic, the teacher had not allowed for the activation of prior knowledge (Pritchard, 2008). The activation of prior knowledge can be defined as "The overall process of assessing individual learners' needs, aptitudes, preferences and prior learning in order to plan and provide an appropriate learning programme to meet their needs" (QIA, 2007: 2).

This can be approached in a number of ways, of course. One way might have been to ask the class certain leading questions; another, more socially constructive approach might have been to ask the class to talk in pairs about certain ideas introduced by the teacher and then gather feedback. Often the construction of a concept map (Novak and Gowin, 1984) in pairs is used to ascertain prior knowledge and understanding. From this the teacher would have gained an insight into the current state of the general knowledge and understanding of the ideas about to be investigated. From this initial assessment the teacher should be able to make a more accurate judgement of an appropriate starting point from which the class could work.

Another notable omission from the lesson was the provision of expert guidance. This can be done in a number of ways, as we have seen, including asking leading questions, providing hints or suggestions and subtly steering ideas and suggestions from the class away from blind alleys. Other scaffolding techniques could also have been employed, such as the provision of written material, possibly worksheets, to complete based on observation and discussion.

The discussion in groups was allowed to be dominated by one idea, which became the only possible explanation considered. A teacher monitoring the groups better would have been able to judge that an intervention at this stage would be quite important and would have taken appropriate steps.

In some cases, allowing learners to observe an event such as the one in this example can serve to stimulate ideas and generate discussion. In this case, this is actually what happened. However, the underlying science of the demonstration was something beyond the understanding of the group. In a case such as this, a commentary, including suggestions, observations and open questions, might well have assisted in the process of coming to understand what was happening. In this case, the observation served to confuse and led to wild ideas being put forward with no safety mechanism to reign in and redirect.

Other supporting activities or demonstrations of a similar nature might also have served to avoid the situation which followed from the demonstration and discussion in groups. For example, the opportunity to see the same event in different ways might have given more observed evidence for the class to think about and think with. In the internet age, where there are countless sites which provide seemingly random events videoed for posterity and given freely for all to use, it is possible to find examples of this demonstration with smaller or much larger containers (including an oil drum, with a very extreme outcome), a version of the demonstration with a soft drink can which is heated and then plunged into cold water and many other examples.

The children's perception of the water causing the can to collapse was a strong one and one which would not easily be displaced. Given the limited experience of the class and given that spraying the hot can with water was a red herring in many respects, this is not wholly surprising. It is likely that an approach from the teacher which included more opportunity for providing some of the social dimensions of learning, some of which are suggested above, might have led to more satisfying outcomes in terms of the experience of the class and the understanding of the underlying scientific principles. This vignette further underlines the importance of the role of the teacher.

Activities

- Compare your teaching practice with one of the vignettes and consider how you could enhance teaching and learning by adopting the pedagogic principles.

- Consider how vignettes representing good teaching practice outside of the context of your teaching could be adapted and made usable by you.

- Considering your own teaching, which aspect of it most closely follows social constructivist principles? How could your teaching be represented by a vignette?

References

ACT (Association for Constructivist Teaching) (2007) Online. Available HTTP: <http://www.odu.edu/educ/act> (accessed 9 September 2009).

Adamse, M. and Motta, S. (2000) *Affairs of the Net: The Cybershrinks' Guide to Online Relationships*. Miami, FL: Health Communications Inc.

Adi, Y., Killoran, A., Janmohamed, K. and Stewart-Brown, S. (2007) *Systematic Review of the Effectiveness of Interventions to Promote Mental Wellbeing in Children in Primary Education. Report 1: Universal Approaches (Non-violence Related Outcomes)*. London: National Institute for Health and Clinical Excellence.

Agar, J., Jones, S. and Simpson, G. (2006) *Teaching Children to Generate Questions Designed to Improve their Capacity to Think Critically about Scientific Questions Standard Site* Online. Available HTTP: <http://www.standards.dfes.gov.uk/ntrp/lib/pdf/questioningscience. pdf > (accessed 9 September 2009).

Alexander, R. (2008) "Culture, dialogue and learning: Notes on an emerging pedagogy" in Mercer, N. and Hodgkinson, S. (eds) *Exploring Talk in School*. London: Sage, 91–114.

Anderson, J. (1983) *The Architecture of Cognition*. Cambridge, MA: Harvard University Press.

Anderson, J. (1990) *Cognitive Psychology and its Implications*, 3rd edition. New York: Freeman.

Anderson, J. (2000) *Cognitive Psychology and its Implications*, 5th edition. New York: Worth Publishers.

Andriessen, J., Baker, M. and Suthers, D. (2003) *Arguing to Learn: Confronting Cognitions in Computer-supported Collaborative Learning Environments*. Dordrecht, Netherlands: Springer.

Armbruster, B. (1996) "Schema theory and the design of content-area textbooks," *Educational Psychologist* 21: 253–276.

Bandura, A. (1977) *Social Learning Theory*. New York: General Learning Press.

Bandura, A. (1986) *Social Foundations of Thought and Action: A Social Cognitive Theory*. New York: Prentice Hall.

Bandura, A. (1997a) *Self-efficacy: The Exercise of Control*. New York: W. H. Freeman.

Bandura, A. (1997b) *Social Learning Theory*. Englewood Cliffs, NJ: Prentice Hall.

Barak, A. and Block, N. (2006) "Factors related to perceived helpfulness in supporting highly distressed individuals through an online support chat," *Cyberpsychology and Behaviour* 9(1).

Bartlett, F. (1932) *Remembering: A Study in Experimental and Social Psychology*. Cambridge: Cambridge University Press.

Bartlett, F. (1958) *Thinking*. New York: Basic Books.

BECTA (British Educational Communications and Technology Agency) (2006) *Using Chat Rooms in the Classroom* Online. Available HTTP: <http://www.becta.org.uk> (accessed 9 September 2009).

Berliner, D. (1998) *Educational Psychology*, 6th edition. Boston and New York: Houghton Mufflin Company.

Bernard, R., Abrami, P., Lou, Y., Borokhovski, E., Wade, A., Wozney L., Wallet, P., Fiset, M. and Huang, B. (2004) "How does distance education compare with classroom instruction? A meta-analysis of the empirical literature," *Review of Educational Research* 74(3): 379–439.

Blair, T. (2003) *Labour Party Conference in Bournemouth*. London: Guardian Online. Available HTTP: <http://http://www.guardian.co.uk/politics/2003/sep/30/labourconference.labour5> (accessed 9 September 2009).

Bransford, J. (1979) *Human Cognition: Learning, Understanding, and Remembering*. Belmont, CA: Wadsworth Publishing.

Brewer, W. and Treyens, J. (1981) "Role of schemata in memory for places," *Cognitive Psychology* 13: 207–230.

Brine, A. (2009) *Language Arts & Disciplines*. London: Ashgate.

Brooks, J. G. and Brooks, M. G. (1993) *In Search of Understanding: The Case for Constructivist Classrooms*. Alexandria, VA: Association for Supervision and Curriculum Development.

Brown, B. (2008) *Key Indicators of Child and Youth Well-being: Completing the Picture*. New York: Lawrence Erlbaum Associates.

Brown, J., Collins, A. and Duguid, P. (1989) "Situated cognition and the culture of learning," *Educational Researcher* 18(1): 32–42.

Bruner, J. (1960) *The Process of Education*. Cambridge, MA: Harvard University Press.

Bruner, J. (1966) *Toward a Theory of Instruction*. Cambridge, MA: Harvard University Press.

Bruner, J. (1973) *Going Beyond the Information Given*. New York: Norton.

Bruner, J. (1983) "Education as social invention," *Journal of Social Issues* 39: 129–141.

Buchanan, A. (2000) "Present issues and concerns" in Buchanan, A. and Hudson, B. (eds) *Promoting Children's Emotional Well-being*. Oxford: Oxford University Press.

Buchanan, A. and Hudson, B. (eds) (2000) *Promoting Children's Emotional Well-being*. Oxford: Oxford University Press.

Burton, D. and Bartlett, S. (2006) "Shaping pedagogy from psychological ideas" in Kassem, D., Mufti, E. and Robinson, J. (eds) *Education Studies: Issues and Critical Perspectives*. Milton Keynes: Open University Press.

Carrier, S. and Moulds, L. (2003) "Pedagogy, andragogy, and cybergogy: Exploring best-practice paradigm for online teaching and learning" presented at Sloan-C Ninth International Conference on Asynchronous Learning Networks (ALN) Orlando, FL Online. Available HTTP: <http://www.sloan-c.org/conference/proceedings/2003/ppt/1471.ppt> (accessed 9 September 2009).

CASEL (2008) *Social and Emotional Learning (SEL) and Student Benefits: Implications for the Safe Schools/Healthy Students Core Elements* Online. Available HTTP: <http://www.casel.org/downloads/EDC_CASELSELResearchBrief.pdf > (accessed 9 September 2009).

Christiansen, H., Krentz, C. and Goulet, L. (2003) "Foreword" in Peter-Koop, A., Santos-Wagner, V., Breen, C. and Begg, A. (eds) *Collaboration in Teacher Education: Examples from the Context of Mathematics Education Volume 1*. Dordrecht, Netherlands: Kluwer Academic Publishers.

Clarke, S. (2001) *Assessment For Learning – TIB WALT WILF OLI* Gillingham: Wigan Schools Online. Available HTTP: <http://www.schoolsonline.wigan.sch.uk> (accessed 9 September 2009).

Clausner, T. and Croft, W. (1997) "Productivity and schematicity in metaphors," *Cognitive Science* 21(3): 247–282.

Coates, J. (1986) *Women, Men and Language.* Harlow: Longman.

Collins, A., Brown, J. and Newman, S. (1989) "Cognitive apprenticeship: Teaching the craft of reading, writing and mathematics" in Resnick, L. B. (ed.) *Knowing, Learning and Instruction: Essays in Honor of Robert Glaser.* Hillsdale, NJ: Erlbaum.

Crook, C. (2000) "Motivation and the ecology of collaborative learning" in Joiner, R., Littleton, K., Faulkner, D. and Miell, D. (eds) *Rethinking Collaborative Learning.* London: Free Association Books.

Danet, B., Wachenhauser, T., Bechar-Israeli, H., Cividalli, A. and Rosenbaum-Tamari, Y. (1995) "Curtain time 20:00 GMT: Experiments with virtual theater on internet relay chat," *Journal of Computer-Mediated Communication* 1(2) Online. Available HTTP: <http://jcmc.indiana.edu/issues.html> (accessed 9 September 2009).

Department for Children, Schools and Families (DCSF) (2008) *Safer Children in a Digital World: The Report of the Byron Review* Online. Available HTTP: <http://publications.dcsf.gov.uk/eOrderingDownload/DCSF-00334-2008.pdf> (accessed 9 September 2009).

DCSF (2009a) *Personalised Learning* Online. Available HTTP: <http://nationalstrategies.standards.dcsf.gov.uk/personalisedlearning> (accessed 9 September 2009).

DCSF (2009b) *The Research Informed Practice Site (TRIPS)* Online. Available HTTP: <http://www.standards.dfes.gov.uk/research/> (accessed 9 September 2009).

Deaux, K., Dane, F. and Wrightsman, L. (1993) *Social Psychology in the '90s,* 6th edition. Pacific Grove, CA: Brooks/Cole Publishing Company.

Deci, E. and Ryan, R. (1985) *Intrinsic Motivation and Self-determination in Human Behaviour.* New York: Plenum Press.

Derry, S. (1999) "A fish called peer learning: Searching for common themes" in O'Donnell, A. and King, A. (eds) *Cognitive Perspectives on Peer Learning.* Hillsdale, NJ: Lawrence Erlbaum Associates.

DfES (2005a) *Excellence and Enjoyment: Social and Emotional Aspects of Learning* Online. Available HTTP: <http://publications.teachernet.gov.uk/eOrderingDownload/DFES0110200 MIG2122.pdf> (accessed 9 September 2009).

DfES (2005b) *Social and Emotional Aspects of Learning: Improving Behaviour, Improving Learning* Online. Available HTTP: <http://nationalstrategies.standards.dcsf.gov.uk/node/87009> (accessed 9 September 2009).

Donaldson, M. (1978) *Children's Minds.* London: Fontana.

Dunkin, M. (1987) *The International Encyclopaedia of Teaching and Teacher Education (Advances in Education).* London: Pergamon.

Elliott, A. (2001) "Introduction" in Richards, M., Elliott, A., Woloshyn, V. and Mitchell, C. (eds) *Collaboration Uncovered: The Forgotten, the Assumed, and the Unexamined in Collaborative Education.* Westport, CT: Bergin & Garvey.

Ernest, P. (1999) *Social Constructivism as a Philosophy of Mathematics: Radical Constructivism* Online. Available HTTP: <http://people.exeter.ac.uk/PErnest/soccon.htm (accessed 15 March 2009).

Eysenck, H. and Eysenck, S. (1969) *Personality Structure and Measurement.* London: Routledge.

Eysenck, M. (2004) *Psychology: An International Perspective*. London: Psychology Press.

Falchikov, N. (2001) *Learning Together: Peer Tutoring in Higher Education*. London: RoutledgeFalmer.

Farrington, D. (1998) "Studying changes within individuals: The causes of offending" in Rutter, M. (ed.) *Studies of Psychosocial Risk: The Power of Longitudinal Data*. Cambridge: Cambridge University Press.

Fisher, R. and Larkin, S. (2005) "Pedagogy or ideological struggle? An examination of pupils' and teachers' expectations for talk in the classroom," *Language and Education* 22(1): 1–16.

Fisher, R. and Larkin, S. (n.d) *An Examination of Pupils' and Teachers' Expectations for Talk in the Classroom*, School of Education and Lifelong Learning, University of Exeter, UK Online. Available HTTP: <http://eric.exeter.ac.uk/exeter/bitstream/10036/40473/1/Pedagogy%20or%20Ideological%20Struggle.pdf> (accessed 9 September 2009).

Fitts, P. and Posner, M. (1967) *Learning and Skilled Performance in Human Performance*. Belmont, CA: Brock Cole.

Freiermuth, M. and Jarrell, D. (2006) "Willingness to communicate: Can online chat help?" *International Journal of Applied Linguistics* 16(2): 189–212.

Freundschuh, S. and Sharma, M. (1996) "Spatial image schemata, locative terms, and geographic spaces," *Children's Narrative: Fostering Spatial Skills in Children Cartographica* 32(2): 38–49.

Gentner, D. and Stevens, A. (1983) *Mental Models*. Hillsdale, NJ: Erlbaum.

Gillies, R. (2007) *Cooperative Learning: Integrating Theory and Practice*. Thousand Oaks, CA: Sage Publications.

von Glasersfeld, E. (1989) "Constructivism in education" in Kusen, T. and Poslethwaite, N. (eds) *International Encyclopaedia of Education* (supplementary volume 162–163). Oxford: Pergamon.

Goleman, D. (1996) *Emotional Intelligence: Why It Can Matter More Than IQ*. London: Bloomsbury.

Goleman, D. (2006) *Emotional Intelligence: 10th Anniversary Edition: Why It Can Matter More Than IQ*. New York: Bantam Publishing.

Gredler, M. (1997) *Learning and Instruction: Theory into Practice*, 3rd edition. Upper Saddle River, NJ: Prentice Hall.

Grigsby, A. (2001) "Let's chat: Chat rooms in the elementary school," *Educational Technology and Society* 4(3): 85–86.

Halliday, M. and Hassan, R. (1989) *Language, Context, and Text: Aspects of Language in a Social-semiotic Perspective*. Oxford: Oxford University Press.

van Harmelen, M. (2008) "Design trajectories: Four experiments in PLE implementation," *Interactive Learning Environments* 16(1): 35–46.

Holland, J., Holyoak, K., Nisbett, R. and Thagard, R. (1986) *Induction: Processes of Inference, Learning and Discovery*. Cambridge, MA: MIT Press.

Hopkins, S. and Lawson, M. (2002) "Explaining the acquisition of a complex skill: Methodological and theoretical considerations uncovered in the study of simple addition and the moving-on process," *Educational Psychology Review* 14(2): 121–154 Online. Available HTTP: <http://tlp.excellencegateway.org.uk/pdf/eng_nat_01.pdf> (accessed 9 September 2009).

Hyslop-Margison, E. and Strobel, J. (2008) "Constructivism and education: misunderstandings and pedagogical implications," *The Teacher Educator* 43(1): 72–86.

Innes, J. (1949) "Some pedagogical implications of wiping a joint," *Journal of Vocational Education & Training* 1(3): 275–280.

Jarvis, P., Griffin, C. and Holford, J. (2003) *The Theory and Practice of Learning*. London: Kogan Page.

Johnson, M. (1987) *The Body in the Mind: The Bodily Basis of Meaning, Imagination and Reason*. Chicago: University of Chicago Press.

Johnson, M. (2008) "Philosophy's debt to metaphor" in Gibbs, R. W. (ed.) *The Cambridge Handbook of Metaphor and Thought*. New York: Cambridge University Press.

Johnson-Laird, P. (1983) *Mental Models*. Cambridge, MA: Harvard University Press.

Joiner, R., Littleton, K., Faulkner, D. and Miell, D. (eds) (2000) *Rethinking Collaborative Learning*. London: Free Association Books.

Kearney, M. (2004) "Classroom use of multimedia-supported predict–observe–explain tasks in a social constructivist learning environment research," *Science Education* 34(4): 427–453.

Kearsley, G. (1996) *Learning with Software: Pedagogies and Practice* Online. Available HTTP: <http://www.educationau.edu.au/archives/cp/default.htm> (accessed 9 September 2009).

Kelly, G. (1963) *Theory of Personality: The Psychology of Personal Constructs*. The Norton Library, London: Norton & Co.

Kelly, G. (1995) *Principles of Personal Construct Psychology*. New York: Norton.

Kent County Council (2004) *Kent ICT* Online. Available HTTP: <http://www.kented.org.uk/ngfl/ict/control/Bee-Bot> (accessed 9 September 2009).

Kirk, G. (1896) *Heraclitus: The Cosmic Fragments*. Cambridge: Cambridge University Press.

Knowles, M. (1970) *The Modern Practice of Adult Education: Andragogy versus Pedagogy*. New York: Association Press.

Knowles, M. (1980) *The Modern Practice of Adult Education: From Pedagogy to Andragogy*. Englewood Cliffs, NJ: Prentice Hall.

Knowles, M. (1990) *The Adult Learner: A Neglected Species*. Houston, TX: Gulf Publishing.

Kolb, D. (1984) *Experiential Learning: Experience as the Source of Learning and Development*. Englewood Cliffs, NJ: Prentice Hall.

Kordaki, M. (2005) "The role of synchronous communication via chat in the formation of e-learning communities," *Proceedings Book of the 3rd International Conference on Multimedia and Information and Communication Technologies in Education m-ICTE2005* Online. Available HTTP: <http://www.formatex.org/micte2006> (accessed 12 July 2009).

Kuhn, W. and Frank, A. (1990) "A formalization of metaphors and image-schemas in user interfaces" in Mark, D. N. and Frank, A. U. (eds) *Cognitive and Linguistic Aspects of Geographic Space*. Las Navas del Marqués, Spain: NATO Advanced Study Institute.

Kukla, A. (2000) *Social Constructivism and the Philosophy of Science*. New York: Routledge.

Lakoff, G. and Johnson, M. (1980) *Metaphors We Live By*. Chicago: University of Chicago Press.

Lave, J. (1988) *Cognition in Practice*. Cambridge: Cambridge University Press.

Lave, J. and Wenger, E. (1991) *Situated Learning: Legitimate Peripheral Participation*. Cambridge: Cambridge University Press.

LeVine, R., Dixon, S., LeVine, S., Richman, A., Leiderman, P., Keefer, C. and Brazelton, T. (1994) *Child Care and Culture: Lessons from Africa*. New York: Cambridge University Press.

Mahoney, J. (2005) "Constructivism and positive psychology" in Snyder, R. and Lopez, S. (eds) *Handbook of Positive Psychology*. Oxford: Oxford University Press.

Mann, C. and Stewart, F. (2000) *Internet Communication and Qualitative Research: A Handbook for Researching Online*. London: Sage.

Marvin, L. (1995) "Spoof, spam, lurk, and lag: The aesthetics of text-based virtual realities," *Journal of Computer-Mediated Communication* 1(2) Online. Available HTTP: <http://jcmc.indiana.edu/vol1/issue2/marvin.html> (accessed 9 September 2009).

McGinnis, E. and Goldstein, A. (1997) *Skillstreaming the Elementary School Child: New Strategies and Perspectives for Teaching Prosocial Skills*, 2nd edition. Champaign, IL: Research Press.

McMahon, M. (1997) "Social constructivism and the World Wide Web: A paradigm for learning," Paper presented at the ASCILITE conference. Perth, Australia.

Mercer, N. and Hodgkinson, S. (2008) *Exploring Talk in School*. London: Sage.

Mercer, N. and Littleton, K. (2007) *Dialogue and the Development of Children's Thinking: A Sociocultural Approach*. London: Routledge.

Mercer, N. and Sams, C. (2006) "Teaching children how to use language to solve maths problems," *Language and Education* Online. Available HTTP: <http://www.informaworld.com/smpp/title~content=t794297816> (accessed 9 September 2009).

Moore, A. (2000) *Teaching and Learning: Pedagogy, Curriculum and Culture*. London: Routledge and Palmer.

National Commission on Excellence in Education (1983) *A Nation At Risk: The Imperative For Educational Reform* Online. Available HTTP: <*http://www.ed.gov/pubs/NatAtRisk*> (accessed 9 September 2009).

National Strategies (2007) *Pedagogy and Personalisation*. London: DfES.

National Strategies (2009) *Intervention in Science* Online. Available HTTP: <http://nationalstrategies.standards.dcsf.gov.uk/search/secondary/results/nav:46403> (accessed 9 September 2009).

Nonnecke, B. and Preece, J. (1999) *Shedding Light on Lurkers in Online Communities*. Proceedings of Ethnographic Studies in Real and Virtual Environments: Inhabited Information Spaces and Connected Communities conference, Edinburgh: 123–128.

Novak, J. and Gowin, D. (1984) *Learning How to Learn*. Cambridge: Cambridge University Press.

Ogle, D. M. (1989) "The know, want to know, learn strategy" in Muth, K. D. (ed.) *Children's Comprehension of Text*. Newark, NY: International Reading Association.

Ormond, J. (1999) *Human Learning*, 3rd edition. Upper Saddle River, NJ: Prentice Hall.

Oxford University Press (2009) *AskOxford Dictionaries* Online. Available HTTP: <http://www.askoxford.com/results/?view=dev_dict&field-12668446=compete> (accessed 9 September 2009).

Peter-Koop, A., Santos-Wagner, V., Breen, C. and Begg, A. (eds) (2003) *Collaboration in Teacher Education: Examples from the Context of Mathematics Education Volume 1*. Dordrecht, Netherlands: Kluwer Academic Publishers.

Piaget, J. (1962) "Comments on Vygotsky's critical remarks concerning *The Language and Thought of the Child,* and *Judgment and Reasoning in the Child*" Tr. Parsons, A.; Tr. and Ed. Hanfmann, E. and Vakar, G. Cambridge: MIT Press Online. Available HTTP: <http://www.marxists.org/archive/vygotsky/works/comment/piaget.htm> (accessed 9 September 2009).

Piaget, J. (1970) *Structuralism*. New York: Harper & Row.

Piaget, J. (1972) *The Psychology of the Child*. New York: Basic Books.

Pickford, S. (2008) "Dimensions of 'vernacular' pedagogy," *English in Education* 22(1): 48–65 Online. Available HTTP: <http://www.informaworld.com/smpp/content~db=all~ content=a907039054> (accessed 9 September 2009).

Prawat, R. (1995) "Misleading Dewey: Reform, projects, and the language game," *Educational Research* 24(7), 13–27.

Prawat, R. and Floden, R. (1994) "Philosophical perspectives on constructivist views of learning," *Educational Psychologist* 29(1), 37–48.

Pritchard, A. (2005) *Ways of Learning*. London: David Fulton.

Pritchard, A. (2009) *Ways of Learning*, 2nd edition. London: Routledge.

Qualifications and Curriculum Authority (QCA) (1999) *The National Curriculum Programmes of Study and Attainment Targets*. London: HMSO.

QCA (2009) *History Key Stage 2: Statutory Content* Online. Available HTTP: <http:// curriculum.qca.org.uk/key-stages-1-and-2/subjects/history/index.aspx> (accessed 9 September 2009).

QIA (2007) *National Teaching and Learning Change Programme* Online. Available HTTP: <http://ntlcp.qia.org.uk/it/documents/aboutqia/glossary.pdf > (accessed 9 September 2009).

Richards, C. (2003) "Chatrooms in the classroom," *InteracTive* 47: 23–25.

Richards, C. (2009) *How Useful Are Bounded Online Chat Rooms as a Source of Pastoral Support in a Sixth-Form College?* University of Southampton, School of Education, Doctoral Thesis. Online. Available HTTP: <http://eprints.soton.ac.uk/66451/> (accessed 9 September 2009).

Richardson, D., Spivey, M., Edelman, S. and Naples, A. (2001) "Language is spatial: Experimental evidence for image schemas of concrete and abstract verbs" in *Proceedings of the Twenty-third Annual Meeting of the Cognitive Science Society*. Mahwah, NJ: Erlbaum.

Robins, L. N. (1986) "Changes in conduct disorder over time" in Farran, D. C. and McKinney, J. D. (eds) *Risk in Intellectual and Physchosocial Development*. New York: Academic Press.

Rohrer, T. (1995) *Feelings Stuck in a GUI Web: Metaphors, Image Schemas and the Human Computer Interface*. Eugene, OR: Center for the Cognitive Science of Metaphor, Philosophy Department, University of Oregon.

Romiszowski, A. (1981) *Designing Instructional Systems: Decision Making in Course Planning and Curriculum Design*. London: Kogan Page.

Roseth, C. J., Johnson, D. W. and Johnson, R. T. (2008) "Promoting early adolescents' achievement and peer relationships: The effects of cooperative, competitive, and individualistic goal structures psychological bulletin," *American Psychological Association* 134(2): 223–246.

Royer, J. (ed.) (2004) *The Cognitive Revolution in Educational Psychology*. Charlotte, NC: Information Age Publishing.

Rutter, M., Giller, H. and Hagell, A. (1998) *Antisocial Behavior by Young People*. Cambridge: Cambridge University Press.

Ryan, R. and Deci, E. (2000) "Self-determination theory and the facilitation of intrinsic motivation, social development, and well-being," *American Psychologist* 55(1): 68–78 Online. Available HTTP: <http://www.psych.rochester.edu/SDT/documents/2000_ RyanDeci_SDT.pdf> (accessed 9 September 2009).

Scopes, L. (2009) *Learning Archetypes as Tools of Cybergogy for a 3D Educational Landscape: A Structure for eTeaching in Second Life*. Southampton: University of Southampton Online. Available HTTP: <http://eprints.soton.ac.uk/66169> (accessed 9 September 2009).

Selby, C. (2009) Does Collaborative Working Between Sixth Form Electronics Students and Computing Students Give Each New Insight into Computing? University of Southampton (unpublished).

Shulman, L. (1987) "Knowledge and teaching: Foundations of the new reform," *Harvard Educational Review* 57: 1–22.

Stewart-Brown, S. (1998) "Public health implications of childhood behaviour problems and parenting programmes" in Buchanan, A. and Hudson, B. (eds) *Parenting, Schooling and Promoting Children's Emotional Well-Being*. Oxford: Oxford University Press.

Stornes, T., Bru, E. and Idsoe, T. (2008) "Classroom social structure and motivational climates: On the influence of teachers' involvement, teachers' autonomy support and regulation in relation to motivational climates in school classrooms," *Scandinavian Journal of Educational Research* 52(3): 315–329 Online. Available HTTP: <http://dx.doi.org/10.1080/003 13830802025124> (accessed 9 September 2009).

Swann, J. and Graddol, D. (1993) "Gender inequalities in classroom talk" in Graddol, D., Maybin, J. and Stierer, B. (eds) *Researching Language and Literacy in Social Context*. Milton Keynes: Open University.

Teach Attention Deficit Hyperactivity Disorder (TADHD) (2009) *Focusing on Instructional Choices*. TADHD Online. Available HTTP: <http://research.aboutkidshealth.ca/ teachadhd/teachingadhd/chapter6#REF48#REF48#>

Teacher Technology Supplies (TTS) (2009) TTS Group www.tts-group.co.uk/Bee-Bot (accessed 12 May 2009).

TIPS (2009) *Constructivist Theory (J. Bruner)* Online. Available HTTP: <http://tip. psychology.org/bruner.html> (accessed 9 September 2009).

Training Development Agency (TDA) (2007) *Professional Standards for Teachers Qualified Teacher Status*. London: TDA.

Tu, C. 2000. "On-line learning migration: From social learning theory to social presence theory in a CMC environment," *Journal of Network and Computer Applications* 23: 27–37.

U.S. Department of Education (2002) *What to Know & Where to Go, Parents' Guide to No Child Left Behind* Online. Available HTTP: <http://www.ed.gov/parents/academic/ involve/nclbguide/parentsguide.pdf> (accessed 9 September 2009).

Veerman, A. (2003) "Constructive discussions through electronic dialogue" in Andriessen, J., Baker, M. and Suthers, D. (eds) *Arguing to Learn: Confronting Cognitions in Computer-Supported Collaborative Learning Environments*. London: Kluwer.

Venkataiah, N. (1998) *Value Education*. New Delhi: APH Publishing Corporation.

Vereijken, B. (1991) *The Dynamics of Skill Acquisition*. Amsterdam, Netherlands: Free University Press.

Vickerstaff, S. (2007) "I was just the boy around the place: What made apprenticeships successful?" *Journal of Vocational Education and Training* 59(3): 331–347.

Vygotsky, L. (1978) *Mind in Society*. Cambridge, MA: Harvard University Press.

Walsh, R. (1999) *Essential Spirituality*. New York: Wiley.

Wang, M. (2007) "Designing online courses that effectively engage learners from diverse cultural backgrounds," *British Journal of Educational Technology* 38(2): 294–311.

Wang, M. and Kang, M. (2006) "Cybergogy for engaged learning: A framework for creating learner engagement through information and communication technology" in Hung, D. and Khine, M. (eds) *Engaged Learning with Emerging Technologies*. Dordrecht, Netherlands: Springer.

Weare, K. and Gray, G. (2003) *What Works in Developing Children's Emotional and Social Competence and Wellbeing?* Online. Available HTTP: <http://www.dcsf.gov.uk/research/data/uploadfiles/RR456.pdf > (accessed 9 September 2009).

Wegerif, R. (2007) *Dialogic Education and Technology: Expanding the Space of Learning.* London: Springer.

Wells, J., Barlow, J. and Stewart-Brown, S. (2002) *A Systematic Review of Universal Approaches to Mental Health Promotion in Schools.* Oxford: University of Oxford Institute of Health Sciences.

Wells, J., Barlow, J. and Stewart-Brown, S. (2003) "A systematic review of universal approaches to mental health promotion in schools," *Health Education* 103(4): 197–220 Online. Available HTTP: <http://www.emeraldinsight.com/0965-4283.htm> (accessed 9 September 2009).

Wertsch, J. (1991) *Voices of the Mind: A Sociocultural Approach to Mediated Action.* Cambridge, MA: Harvard University Press.

Wight, M. and Chapparo, C. (2008) "Social competence and learning difficulties: Teacher perceptions," *Australian Occupational Therapy Journal* 55(4): 256–265.

Willett, R. and Sefton-Green, J. (2003) "Living and learning in chatrooms (or does informal learning have anything to teach us?)," *Éducation et Sociétés* (2) English version Online. Available HTTP: <http://www.wac.co.uk/sharedspaces/chatrooms.pdf> (accessed 9 September 2009).

Williams, L. (1999) "But, isn't that cheating? [collaborative programming]," *Frontiers in Education*, 2, 29th Annual Frontiers in Education Conference.

Winer, M. and Ray, K. (1994) *Collaboration Handbook, Creating, Sustaining and Enjoying the Journey.* St Paul, MN: Wilder Foundation.

Woolfolk, A. (1993*) Educational Psychology*. Needham Heights, MA: Allyn and Bacon.

Woollard, J. (2004a) *Image-Schemas as Diagrams* Online. Available HTTP: <http://www.cblt.soton.ac.uk/metaphor/image-schema> (accessed 9 September 2009).

Woollard, J. (2004b) "Pedagogic content knowledge – not just knowing it but knowing how to teach it," *InteracTive* 50: 17.

Wray, D. and Lewis, M. (1997) *Extending Literacy.* London: Routledge.

Zins, J., Bloodworth, M., Weissberg, R. and Walberg, H. (2004) "The scientific base linking social and emotional learning to school success" in *Building Academic Success on Social and Emotional Learning: What Does the Research Say?* Teachers College, Columbia University Online. Available HTTP: <http://www.casel.org/downloads/T3053c01.pdf> (accessed 9 September 2009).

Index